T0334544

GLOBAL DEVELOPMENT

How do we try to make the world a better place, when the challenges of poverty, disease, war, conflict, and climate change continue to impact millions of lives? *Global Development: The Basics* is a lively and engaging introduction to the shifting landscape of global development, right from its origins, to present-day problems, and on to what the future for global development might look like.

Recognising global development as an economic, political, and social project, this book tackles a series of critical questions: asking 'what' development is and how it is measured, where and to whom it is assumed to happen, how its approaches are developed, and whose benefit do they serve? The book invites readers to consider the complexities and challenges of the concept of development, including its historical roots in colonialism, and the geopolitical power relations which continue to set much of the agenda. It investigates whose voices are included or silenced in dominant approaches to development, and the growing importance of 'non-traditional' development funding and approaches.

Covering key topics in the field, from economics and politics, through to gender and climate change, *Global Development: The Basics* is perfect for readers starting out in their understanding of global development.

Daniel Hammett is Senior Lecturer in political and development geography at the Department of Geography, University of Sheffield, UK, and a Senior Research Fellow at the Department of Geography, Environmental Management and Energy Studies,

University of Johannesburg. His work focuses on the intersections of citizenship, popular geopolitics, and global development and has been published in journals including *Political Geography, International Development Planning Review, Progress in Human Geography,* and *Citizenship Studies.*

The Basics

The Basics is a highly successful series of accessible guidebooks which provide an overview of the fundamental principles of a subject area in a jargon-free and undaunting format.

Intended for students approaching a subject for the first time, the books both introduce the essentials of a subject and provide an ideal springboard for further study. With over 50 titles spanning subjects from Artificial Intelligence to Women's Studies, *The Basics* are an ideal starting point for students seeking to understand a subject area.

Each text comes with recommendations for further study and gradually introduces the complexities and nuances within a subject.

Other titles in the series can be found at: https://www.routledge.com/The-Basics/book-series/B

GLOBAL DEVELOPMENT
THE BASICS

Daniel Hammett

Routledge
Taylor & Francis Group

LONDON AND NEW YORK

Designed cover image: © Getty Images

First published 2024
by Routledge
4 Park Square, Milton Park, Abingdon, Oxon OX14 4RN

and by Routledge
605 Third Avenue, New York, NY 10158

Routledge is an imprint of the Taylor & Francis Group, an informa business

© 2024 Daniel Hammett

The right of Daniel Hammett to be identified as author of this work has been asserted in accordance with sections 77 and 78 of the Copyright, Designs and Patents Act 1988.

British Library Cataloguing-in-Publication Data
A catalogue record for this book is available from the British Library

ISBN: 978-0-367-72632-4 (hbk)
ISBN: 978-0-367-72631-7 (pbk)
ISBN: 978-1-003-15565-2 (ebk)

DOI: 10.4324/9781003155652

Typeset in Bembo
by Taylor & Francis Books

CONTENTS

ILLUSTRATIONS

FIGURES

TABLES

BOXES

ABBREVIATIONS

AI	Amnesty International
BRICS	Brazil, Russia, India, China, South Africa (grouping of five leading emerging economies, acronym emerged in 2001)
CCT	Conditional Cash Transfer
CIVETS	Colombia, Indonesia, Vietnam, Egypt, Turkey, South Africa (grouping of six emerging economies, acronym emerged in 2009)
COP	UN Climate Change Conference of Parties
CPAG	Child Poverty Action Group
CSO	Civil Society Organisation
DAC	Development Assistance Committee
EDC	Economically Developed Country
ELDC	Economically Less Developed Country
EMDC	Economically More Developed Country
EPZ	Export Processing Zone
EU	European Union
FAO	Food and Agricultural Organization
GAD	Gender And Development
GATT	General Agreement on Tariffs and Trade
GDP	Gross Domestic Product
GDP PPP	Gross Domestic Product Purchasing Power Parity
GNI	Gross National Income
GNP	Gross National Product
G7	Group of 7 (intergovernmental political forum comprising Canada, France, Germany, Italy, Japan, United Kingdom, United States of America)

G77	Group of 77 (alternative intergovernmental political forum to the G7, comprising 134 countries)
HDI	Human Development Index
HIPC	Heavily Indebted Poor Country
HRW	Human Rights Watch
ICT	Information Communication Technology
IFI	International Financial Institution
IMF	International Monetary Fund
INGO	International Non-Governmental Organisation
IPCC	Intergovernmental Panel on Climate Change
ISI	Import Substitution Industrialisation
MDG	Millennium Development Goal
MDPI	Multi-Dimensional Poverty Index
MINTS	Mexico, Indonesia, Nigeria, Turkey (grouping of countries seen as having potential for rapid economic growth)
MNC	Multinational Corporation
MSF	Médecins sans Frontières
NAM	Non-Aligned Movement
NGO	Non-Governmental Organisation
OCHA	Office for the Coordination of Humanitarian Assistance
ODA	Overseas Development Assistance
OECD	Organisation for Economic Co-operation and Development
OPEC	Organisation of Petroleum Exporting Countries
PRSP	Poverty Reduction Strategy Paper
REDD	Reducing Emissions from Deforestation and forest Degradation
SAIH	Norwegian Students and Academics' International Fund
SAP	Structural Adjustment Programme
SDG	Sustainable Development Goal
TNC	Transnational Corporation
UCT	Unconditional Cash Transfer
UN	United Nations
UNDP	United Nations Development Programme
UNHCR	United Nations High Commission for Refugees
UNICEF	United Nations Children Fund

USAID	US Agency for International Development
USSR	Union of Soviet Socialist Republics
WAD	Women And Development
WB	World Bank
WCED	World Commission on Environment and Development
WFP	World Food Programme
WHO	World Health Organization
WID	Women In Development
WTO	World Trade Organization

ACKNOWLEDGEMENTS

Writing this book has been a slow process, one that has spanned three British Prime Ministers, four Chancellors of the Exchequer, two COP summits, and the joint hottest British summer on record. As ever, the journey of writing a book has taken unexpected twists and turns. I am incredibly fortunate to have been supported by many people along the way.

I would like to thank Lucy and Euan for their love and support throughout the journey. I also extend my thanks for previous and current research and teaching collaborators who, whether knowingly or not, have informed my thinking on various of the topics covered in this book. I also really appreciate the input of Sarah Bickerstaff for thoughts and comments on the final draft of the work. Thanks are also due to the team at Routledge who stuck with me through this process, in particular Helena Hurd, Rosie Anderson, and Katerina Lade.

GLOBAL DEVELOPMENT – MAKING A DIFFERENCE?

What is the first image or idea that comes to mind when someone mentions global development? Is it the logos or names of major international charities and non-governmental organisations (NGOs) such as Oxfam, Médecins sans Frontières (MSF), or the Red Cross and Red Crescent? Is it key governmental departments and donors such as the US Agency for International Development (USAID) or the UK's Foreign, Commonwealth and Development Office? Is it a vision of an aid worker delivering medical or logistical support in a refugee camp? Is it an image of someone taking water from a river or waiting to receive food aid? A picture of office workers poring over spreadsheets and action plans?

If you were given a world map and asked to colour in those countries which are 'developed' and those which are 'developing', which countries would these be? Why would you make these choices? What if you were asked to rank a series of countries (for instance France, Mexico, Italy, Argentina, Cuba, South Africa, Morocco, Thailand, Singapore, Fiji, and Rwanda) in order of development; what would the order be and why? What information would you use to make these decisions?

As this book will explore, global development encompasses a vast array of activities, actors, ideals, and representations. The ways in which global development is understood and approached – in policy, practice, and research – have changed over time, reflecting changing global political priorities and agendas, economic conditions, and other factors. In simple terms we can see these changes reflected in the differing ways in which development is talked

DOI: 10.4324/9781003155652-1

about and located, as well as through the use of different indicators to define and measure development needs and poverty.

Fundamentally, the emergence of global development as a field of work and study was rooted in a belief that some 'countries and societies were/are lagging behind – i.e. underdeveloped – compared to other regions of the world. Historically, these ideas were linked to ideas of 'civilisation' and 'modernity' of the Enlightenment period. This Eurocentric, Western-biased view positioned the countries of Europe, Scandinavia, and North America as beacons of development and modernisation to which other countries should be supported in aspiring to be like. These narratives are profoundly powerful and political, creating perceptions not only of *who* is developed and *who* needs to be developed, but also of *how* development should happen and *who can help* in realising development outcomes.

This book sets out to think about a series of related questions and the assumptions that frame common responses: What is development? Where and to whom do we assume development happens? Who decides what development means and who benefits? Who 'does' development? In answering these questions you will encounter a confusing array of acronyms and abbreviations. Do you know your MINTS from your CIVETS? Your BRICS from your G77? To help you wade through this alphabet-soup, a full list of the acronyms and abbreviations used in this book can be found in the list of abbreviations.

WHAT IS DEVELOPMENT?

As the rest of this book demonstrates, development is a changing and contested term. However, it is useful to have a foundational starting point for the later discussions. So, what do we mean by development? And from this, how do we measure development?

As a starting point, we can think of development as both a goal and a process. The *Oxford English Dictionary* (OED Online, 2023) defines development as 'the action or process of bringing something to a fuller or more advanced condition', 'the economic and social advancement of a country, region, etc, esp. one in the developing world', *and* 'the state or condition of being developed'. In other words, when we talk of development we are often referring both to the processes of change *and* to the outcomes of these processes. Inherently, change involves both a starting point (the current level of development) and the intended and realised endpoint (the aspired-to and realised level of development), as well as the processes of change. These processes, as this book explores, are laden with power and politics, are often contested, and can have both positive and negative, intended and unintended outcomes.

Fundamentally, the meaning of what development *is* remains hotly contested. A useful way of thinking about development can be taken from geographer Rob Potter's (2001: 423) understanding of development as:

> improving the lot of the bulk of the population, then it is implicit that this will entail reductions in both relative and absolute poverty ... [improve] access to non-pecuniary benefits, such as freedom of speech, self-expression and effective participation ... [and] should be synonymous with the advancement of social democracy as a whole.

While Potter offers a relatively positive framing of development, we can contrast this with a more pessimistic view from Gilbert Rist (2007: 488), that 'the essence of "development" is the general transformation and destruction of the natural environment and of social relations in order to increase the production of commodities (goods and services) geared, by means of market exchange, to effective demand'.

These contrasting views highlight a series of key themes. First, development is assumed to be about progress, growth, and advancement. This is certainly the language used to promote global development policies and practices. In reality, **development is not always experienced as progressive, and certainly not as a smooth, linear path to advancement**. On too many occasions, development has been a damaging concept – one that has exacerbated inequalities, created poverty, disenfranchised populations, and ultimately may lead to the destruction of the planet.

Major infrastructure development projects – such as hydro-electric power dams, new shipping ports or airports, coal or mineral mines, large-scale solar-power projects, or transport corridors – may be seen as vital to national-level economic development agendas. But such initiatives require vast amounts of land, often resulting in the displacement of communities from their lands, livelihoods, and cultural heritage. Estimates suggest that 15 million people are displaced from their homes each year due to such large-scale development projects (Horta, 2020). From the Narmada River dams in India, to the Three Gorges Dam in China (which is estimated to have displaced 1.3 million people alone), to the expansion of solar-power plants in the Oaxaca province of Mexico, such mega-projects may attract international donor support and funding while being positioned as integral to national development. But they have and can cause untold costs and suffering at the local level as communities are forced to relocate and abandon homes and land, as well as emotional and cultural connections, as lands are submerged by reservoirs or paved over to support massive energy installations.

Recent development projects, presented as being nature- and sustainability-focused, can also lead to the displacement of populations and exclusion of peoples from traditional lands and livelihoods – as seen in 2022 with Maasai communities being forcibly removed from their traditional lands in the Ngorongoro Conservation Area in Tanzania. The removal and exclusion of communities from their lands in the name of conservation – a phenomenon often talked about as 'fortress conservation' (Brockington, 2002) – has roots in colonial-era practices of land appropriation and remains integral to development agendas (often linked to tourism-led development approaches) in many countries.

This is not to say that we should accept the status quo. Rather we need to think critically about how we approach and understand the concept of development in a holistic and sustainable way while recognising and overcoming colonial legacies and Western biases. Hence, second, we need to ask **who defines and how do we measure development?** As chapter 3 outlines, this idea is contested and not all agree on what constitutes 'developed', and questions remain about the scale at which advancement should be measured (local, national, regional, global) and against what indicators (social, economic, political, environmental). Third, what is the spatiality – the geography – that is already assumed? As the following chapters highlight, **global development is not just something that is important or needed 'out there'** but is a *global* concern and continued popular assumptions and representations of development as only a matter for the global south are not only false but a continued form of colonialism.

Perhaps the most common starting point in popular discussions of global development – and therefore the most common definition of development – is poverty and poverty reduction. The majority of the world's population live in poverty: 600 million people currently live in extreme poverty (a household income of less than $1.90 per day), the vast majority in African countries. While this figure represents a massive drop in the numbers living in extreme poverty over the past 30 years, from 1.9 billion (or 36% of the world's population) in 1990, it is only a partial story. While global economic growth and the expansion of an emergent middle class have driven this decline, the headline figure has been skewed by extensive economic growth in one particular country: China. The realities of poverty reduction are complex and uneven. The poorest and most vulnerable have generally been left behind and entrenched geographical inequalities remain as extreme poverty has become concentrated in a number of African countries. More broadly, the increasing inequalities in wealth between the world's richest 1% and the rest indicate increasing socio-economic polarisation. In addition, the impacts of climate change, geopolitical tensions (including the war in Ukraine), and legacies of Covid-19 challenge the potential for economic growth and poverty reduction.

It is vital, however, not to reduce discussion of the successes, failures, and challenges in tackling (extreme) poverty to simple economics. Through much of the latter half of the twentieth century, global development agendas prioritised economic growth as *the* magic bullet or holy grail for poverty reduction. This privileging of economics was exemplified by the United Nations' (UN's) argument that:

> rapid economic progress is impossible without painful adjustments. Ancient philosophies have to be scrapped; old social institutions have to disintegrate; bonds of caste, creed and race have to burst; and large numbers of people who cannot keep up with progress have to have their expectations of a comfortable life frustrated.

> (UN, 1951)

In other words, economic growth was equated to development (and vice versa) and society, culture, and other norms were expected to change to support this agenda.

As we explore in chapter 2, the failure of this economic-centric approach has resulted in a gradual shift to a more holistic view of development. By 1975 the UN was arguing that:

> The ultimate end of development is to achieve a better quality of life for all, which means not only the development of economic and other material resources but also the physical, moral, intellectual and cultural growth of the human person.
>
> (UN, 1976)

Over the intervening years approaches to development have continued to evolve and engage with the human development, capabilities, and sustainable development approaches (discussed further in chapters 2 and 3). Awareness of the importance of sustainable development has never been higher – think of the coverage of recent COP summits, the Fridays for Future school climate strikes, and the Sustainable Development Goals (SDGs). Preceding current attention on the lasting impacts of humanity's unsustainable use of the planet, the Brundtland Commission report (Brundtland, 1987) provided a defining moment at which the impact of development and economic growth upon the environment began to gain international political attention. These concerns have accelerated as the impacts of climate change intensify. However while recent COP summits have sought to secure binding global agreements on reaching net-zero carbon emissions and restricting global average temperature rise to a maximum of 1.5 degrees Celsius, these efforts remain frustrated by national governments' prioritising short-term economic growth over the necessity for (global) environmental sustainability.

Adopting a more holistic approach to global development also requires a more nuanced means of measuring development. Simple economic indicators such as poverty rates and GDP (Gross Domestic Product) are often used as proxies for development. However, these are inadequate and incomplete (see chapter 3), and measures of development have diversified to include non-economic factors in the Human Development Index (HDI) and the

Multi-Dimensional Poverty Index (MDPI). The emergence of the Millennium (MDGs) and then Sustainable Development Goals (SDGs), and monitoring of progress towards these, have resulted in a rapid expansion in the data industry around global development. While this obsession with data means we can discuss progress towards SDGs' targets in detail, has this resulted in a focus on results over process, on achieving short-term successes without tackling underlying structural inequalities? Do these data — and our use of them — continue to perpetuate imagined geographies of where development needs to happen?

WHERE DOES DEVELOPMENT HAPPEN?

The correct answer is everywhere. The false, but more common, answer is 'over there'. This dominant narrative creates a duality between the West ('us') and the rest ('them'), the 'developed' and 'developing' or 'less developed' worlds. From US President Truman's 1949 inauguration speech (which is seen as the start of the contemporary development paradigm and the 'discovery' of mass poverty) to the present, the popular perception remains that development is a concern 'elsewhere' — namely in the global south.

This imagined geography of global development continues to be reproduced through the language and practices of development. As the anti-development theorist Arturo Escobar (1999) argues, the global south is continually produced and reconstructed by Western actors as the 'other' against which the West is positioned as modern and developed. While efforts have been made to challenge this imagined geography, the success of making global development truly *global* has been limited — despite the policy shift from the MDGs (development goals for the global south only) to the SDGs (globally applicable targets and goals, with *all* countries having targets to meet). While this change was applauded at the time has it really led to changes in everyday perception and political practice? When was the last time you heard of domestic policy in the UK, France, or Spain being framed in terms of the SDGs? Do mainstream media ever mention German, Australian, or Canadian progress towards their SDG targets? Finding such examples is about as easy as finding hen's teeth.

You can, though, find data on Western countries' progress towards SDG indicators relatively easily. For the UK, you can find this at https://sdgdata.gov.uk/ – but be warned, it makes for sombre reading with little evidence of progress towards many SDG targets. Overall, this lack of popular and political will in thinking about development as happening 'here' not only reflects a failure of Western leaders to substantively buy into the *global* of global development but also perpetuates the myth that development is something that happens in geographically distant places and to other people. Who those people are and where they live brings us to thinking about the language of development.

THE CHANGING LANGUAGE OF DEVELOPMENT

So, should you talk about international development or global development? Of First World and Third World? Of majority and minority worlds? Of the global north and global south? Of more and less economically developed countries? The changing language we use to talk about development is important – it tells us about the evolving history, politics, and geographies of the idea; it also conjures up images and imaginaries of peoples, places, presents, and futures (see Cornwall, 2007).

The initial language of development was rooted in Cold War geopolitics, dividing the world into three blocs: the capitalist First World (North America, Western Europe, Scandinavia, Japan, Australia, and South Korea), the communist Second World (Soviet Union (USSR), Cuba, China, Eastern Europe, and other socialist states), and the Third World (decolonising and newly decolonised states in Africa, Asia, Latin America, and the Caribbean). This terminology not only provided a spatial representation of who was seen as being developed or in need of development, but gave rise to understandings and representations of people and places in specific ways – as modern or backwards, as civilised or primitive. The Third World then quickly became the subject of geopolitical strategies of the two geopolitical superpowers – the USA and the USSR – whose 'development' policies were generally tied to geopolitical agendas and military interests, often at the expense of social justice and human rights.

By the 1980s, development debates began to include the language of 'developed' and 'developing' countries. At this time the publication of the influential Brandt Report argued that the world was primarily divided by economics, with the wealth of the rich north accruing from manufacturing industry profits while the poor south was reliant upon primary commodity exports. While the Brandt Report called for a process of wealth redistribution and a move to a more equitable global political economy, its more lasting impact has been through a powerful visual representation which became common in international development circles: the Brandt Line. This line, based upon the GDP per capita of each country, provided a simple and accessible visualisation of the world as divided between the 'economically developed' north and 'underdeveloped' south, entrenching a popular, imagined geography of development.

The dominance of economics-based approaches to development was further evidenced in the World Bank's (WB's) classification system for countries: as 'developing' (low and middle income), 'industrialised' (primarily members of the Organisation for Economic Co-operation and Development (OECD) plus South Africa, but excluding Greece, Portugal, Spain, and Turkey), or 'capital-surplus oil-exporting' countries (Nielsen, 2011: 11). In 1989, the WB moved to a new set of terms – low-, lower-middle-, upper-middle-, and high-income countries – officially moving away from the term developing country (although the term remained in use due to 'convenience' (Nielsen, 2011)).

During the 1990s, the language of development shifted again. The ending of the Cold War pre-empted a major global geopolitical realignment, leading to the demise of the First/Second/Third World terminology. The terms 'developed' and 'developing' world were also replaced with the language of Economically Developed (or Economically More Developed) and Economically Less Developed Countries (EDCs or EMDCs and ELDCs). This emphasis on economics reflected the neoliberal world-order and continued privileging economic growth as *the* key driver of development.

By the 2000s and 2010s, momentum was growing for further changes in the language of development. Terms including global north and global south, and minority and majority worlds became more common. These changes attempted to move beyond discrete, binary developed/developing categories. However, critics cautioned that the global south/north terminology risked an inadvertent spatial fetishisation of where development has or needs to happen, and the continued assumption that the 'south' is inferior and in need of development. The use of minority and majority worlds thus sought distance from an imagined geography of development, while emphasising the continued privilege and power of the few (minority world) and marginalisation and exploitation of the many (majority world).

In 2014 the Bill and Melinda Gates Foundation argued, 'the world has changed so much that the terms "developing countries" and "developed countries" have outlived their usefulness' (Gates and Gates, 2014: 5) while the WB discontinued use of global north/south and developed/developing countries in 2015, instead reporting data by geographical regions (Khokhar and Serajuddin, 2015). Similarly, the World Health Organization (WHO) works by geographical regions, grouping high-income countries into one 'region' while low- and middle-income countries are grouped into 6 regional areas.

The terminology of developed and developing countries has however remained in common use by the UN and the World Trade Organization (WTO). UN agencies adopt differing definitions – from the 'common practice' definition of UNStats (2013), 'In common practice, Japan in Asia, Canada and the United States in northern America, Australia and New Zealand in Oceania, and Europe are considered "developed" regions', to the UN Development Programme's (UNDP's) defining of developed countries as the top 25% according to the Human Development Index (HDI). Adopting a different approach, the WTO allows countries to declare whether they are 'developed' or 'developing' whereas the International Monetary Fund (IMF) talks of 36 'advanced economies' and 153 'emerging market and developing economies'.

Ultimately, the language of development reflects the continued dominance of the global north (scholars, policy makers, institutions) in defining what development is, how it is measured, where it is needed and by whom, and how it should be realised (Escobar, 1999; Hammett, 2019; Willis, 2014). These practices mean that the developmental experience of the West remains the expected pathway for all, overlooking histories of colonial expansionism and exploitation, while the language of development remains imbued with (often racialised) binary understandings and representations of 'us' (the developed) and 'them' (the developing) (Biccum, 2011; Kothari, 2006).

WHY DOES DEVELOPMENT MATTER?

We might like to think that development matters because we care for the health and well-being of both our fellow humans and our shared planet. This altruistic vision certainly matters for many. However, a cynic would say development matters because it is big business. The global development sector employs millions of people around the world, involving the transfer and spending of billions of dollars a year – and that's just in terms of overseas development assistance (ODA), and the charity and non-profit sector. Add to this the billions of dollars of remittances sent around the world each year, as well as non-ODA loans, and national government spending, and development really is big business.

Development is also a politically and economically powerful concept. Imposing global development agendas and priorities can cause wholesale political and social changes within a country – as seen in the imposition of Structural Adjustment Programmes (SAPs) on debtor states by the World Bank during the 1990s. Meanwhile, national governments can – and do – use the need for national development and economic growth to force through particular policies and projects. Defended as being 'in the national interest', large-scale infrastructural projects can have profound negative impacts on local populations (who may be displaced) and environments (which may be destroyed).

Governments also mobilise the promise of development to sell themselves to voters on the promise of a better tomorrow: of economic growth, job creation, better working conditions, improved service delivery, and infrastructure development. In return, successfully elected political leaders often 'repay' supporters with targeted investments in particular regions and constituencies. Make no mistake, these practices are not – as stereotypes would have you believe – confined to autocratic and authoritarian leaders in the global south and can be seen in the distribution of national development funds and other resources in various countries in the global north, including the UK.

On an international level, the term development also does a lot of (geo)political work. It is used to justify foreign policy decisions and is tied to dominant political ideologies, as seen in the neo-liberal turn of the 1980s. It is used to leverage support and votes in key international political forums (what is known as 'soft power' on the political stage) and to secure favourable access to export markets or to natural resources and energy supplies. The 'new scramble for Africa', which has seen concerted efforts by China to expand development engagements, political alliances, and resource access across the continent – as well as Western concerns with and responses to this – highlights the entwining of global development with national development and geopolitical agendas (Carmody, 2016).

Elsewhere, development is used to mobilise agendas for social justice. Leftist and indigenous political leaders in Bolivia and elsewhere have offered alternative national development agendas and approaches, placing indigenous values and social justice at the heart of their endeavours. Many civil society organisations (CSOs) and campaign groups inherently link development campaigns to the quest for social justice (the seeking of a more equitable spread of 'goods' and 'bads' across societies, be this in terms of environmental security, equitable access to education, or tackling gender-based violence).

Others argue that development matters because it continually fails to deliver on stated goals and aims, instead entrenching existing inequalities. Anti-development scholars such as Arturo Escobar (1995: 5) have argued that despite ubiquitous efforts to promote development programmes throughout the late twentieth century, 'The fact that most people's conditions not only did not improve but deteriorated with the passing of time did not seem to bother most experts.' More recently Dambisa Moyo (2009) has argued that current development approaches have failed to promote sustained economic growth while entrenching corruption and bad governance, and Maggie Black (2007) contends that development initiatives have undermined the realisation of human rights and entrenched inequalities.

Ultimately, development matters across a range of scales (local, national, global) and in numerous ways (as political agenda, as economic practice, as ideological tool) and has direct impacts on people's lives. Underpinning these concerns are questions as to whose responsibility is global development? To whom is this responsibility owed, and by whom is this responsibility held? What is this responsibility for and why does this responsibility exist? These are questions we begin to explore in the next few chapters. The answers to these questions are not always clear-cut and often remain infused with colonial imaginaries and legacies.

DECOLONISING DEVELOPMENT

The legacies of colonialism sit at the heart of global development – from the imagined geographies of where development needs to happen, through the location of key development institutions' headquarters, to the policies and practices of global development in daily life. As Diane Liverman (2018: 168) succinctly argues, global development has 'roots in the colonial enterprise to exploit natural resources and "civilize" non-Western cultures', resulting in a focus on 'modernisation' (i.e. Westernisation) and economic growth.

Recent scandals surrounding sexual abuse and inequitable treatment of local and expatriate staff by major international organisations, including Oxfam, have shone a light into the daily practices of the development sector. Building on momentum from the Black Lives Matter movement, organisations including Peace Direct (2021) have argued that it is *Time to Decolonise Aid*. As their report makes clear, the global development sector remains dominated by global north institutions and power holders, whose policies and everyday practices often remain rooted in structural racism – from the differential treatment of local and expatriate staff to the use of language that perpetuates stereotypes and reinforces 'white saviour' mindsets.

Anti- and post-development scholars have long argued that global development is a self-serving political creation of the global north. The 1955 Bandung conference and growth of the Non-Aligned Movement (NAM) indicate longstanding unease with the political power of the global north and continued influence of former colonial powers over (newly) independent states. Critics have argued that development is simply a new form of imperialism, mobilised via economic, political, social, and cultural power and continually creating both a need for (a certain kind of) development and a collective imaginary of who it is who can offer and who needs this support.

These power dynamics are perpetuated through a set of knowledges, stereotypes, structures, and processes which reinforce colonial-era assumptions of superiority and inferiority. Decolonising development therefore requires the dismantling of these narratives alongside a rebalancing of power away from the global north in determining what development looks like, how it might be achieved, who has agency, which goals are prioritised, and in whose interests decisions are made (Peace Direct, 2021).

While this book is not specifically about decolonising development it will give you an initial sense of both the historical, colonial precedent for the contemporary global development context and the complex legacies of these histories. From this, you will begin to understand how and why global development perpetuates colonialism, and the importance of moves to decolonise the sector.

KEY INTERNATIONAL INSTITUTIONS

Institutions matter in global development. Institutions are not simply bodies such as the United Nations (UN) or a Ministry for Education but include the 'set[s] of rules, written or informal, governing relationships among role occupants in social organisations' (Portes, 2012: 7). In other words, institutions can be understood as encompassing everything from the household (an institution in which decisions are made about access to services, or about prioritisation in the use of financial or other resources) through to national and international organisations.

Major international institutions are central to determining and defining what development is, where development needs to happen, how development should occur, and – ultimately – how development outcomes are measured. The UN remains at the forefront of these discussions and policies. Established in 1945 with a remit to support the maintaining of global political and military stability, and economic and social advancement, the UN comprises 193 member states (all undisputed independent states excluding the Vatican City) and 2 non-member 'observer' states (The Holy See (which oversees the Vatican City) and the State of Palestine). Within the UN, the Economic and Social Council has responsibility for supporting development endeavours through subsidiary bodies including the High-Level Political Forum on Sustainable Development.

Another key global institution whose policies directly influence global development is the World Trade Organization (WTO). Founded as the General Agreement on Tariffs and Trade (GATT) in 1948, the WTO was established to regulate and promote free international trade and sets legally binding rules on all member states (including the removal of protectionist legislation – laws introduced by countries to protect their own producers and manufacturers from competition from international suppliers). However, critics of the WTO have highlighted policy biases in favour of the global north, a lack of accountability, and failures to protect human rights and the environment.

Other major institutions dominate the development funding landscape – in particular Bretton Woods Institutions (so named because they were conceived at a conference in Bretton Woods, USA in 1944). The most high-profile of these organisations are the International Monetary Fund (IMF) which was set up to provide short-term support and finance to states in the face of immediate instability, and the World Bank (tasked with providing longer-term financial support for development). The adoption of the neoliberal economic consensus by these institutions during the 1980s (see chapter 4) resulted in the implementation of an ideologically rooted development agenda – one which continues to permeate the policies of the Bretton Woods Institutions to this day.

Due to their power, critics ask to whom are these institutions accountable? They are not elected by national populations; key positions and boards are often dominated by appointments from the global north and voting systems are often weighted in favour of countries from the global north. While each member state of the UN has a vote on resolutions, each of the 5 permanent members of the security council (China, France, Russia, UK, US) retains the power to veto UN resolutions. Meanwhile, the IMF decision-making is based upon a quota system wherein each member state has a quota of votes based upon how much it pays to the IMF. This so-called 'one-dollar one-vote' approach means wealthier countries have more votes and more power. This power imbalance is further entrenched in the membership of the IMF Executive Board – the group responsible for the daily running and decisions of the IMF. This group is made up of 24 executive directors, including representatives for 8 individual countries (China, France, Germany, Japan, Russia, Saudi Arabia, UK, US) and 16 'blocks' or 'constituencies' comprising multiple countries. Once the quotas of votes are tallied up, the US holds 16.5% of votes, followed by Japan (6.14%), China (6.08%), and Germany (5.31%) – compared to the 11.77% held collectively by **all** Middle Eastern, North African, and sub-Saharan African states combined (of which, Saudi Arabia alone accounts for 2.01%) (IMF, 2021).

It is not just these global bodies that carry influence – major global brands and companies (multinational and transnational corporations (MNCs and TNCs)) are also key players in global development. Often wielding financial clout in excess of the national budgets of smaller nations, MNCs and TNCs have proven adept at pressuring national governments to waive environmental, human rights, tax, and other laws in return for their 'investment'. While lacking the same economic clout as TNCs and MNCs, International NGOs (INGOs) are also powerful actors in global development. This power may be in terms of investigating and reporting on various issues and seeking to hold governments accountable (e.g. Human Rights Watch (HRW), Amnesty International (AI)), influencing (inter)national development agendas, and/or through their role in direct provision of service delivery (e.g. Save the Children, Oxfam).

The central importance of national-level institutions in defining and implementing development priorities must also be recognised. National institutions – including government ministries – are lynchpins for development (Portes and Smith, 2012), but are often either marginalised by donors or under-resourced. Capacity challenges of state institutions (historically due to the failure of withdrawing colonial powers to adequately plan for and support their exit from state institutions, and more recently due to donor demands for a 'rolling back' of the state and reduction in government spending) remain key limits to development.

Domestic NGOs, community-based organisations, trade unions, and other collectives are also vital to the realisation of global development agendas. These organisations are increasingly integral to service delivery, advocacy and support work for marginalised communities as well as human and environmental rights, and efforts to promote good governance. Despite the progressive potential of civil society organisations (CSOs), it is important to remember that some CSOs can also be highly conservative and exclusionary. Furthermore, the role of CSOs in national development may also be contested by national governments and international donors. Advocates for civil society argue that these organisations are vital in strengthening democracy and holding states accountable. However, many governments are resistant to the 'watchdog' role of civil society and have introduced legislation to confine the role of CSOs to supporting state-backed agendas and service delivery. Meanwhile, caution is needed to avoid parachuting Western ideas of civil society into other contexts and (inadvertently) perpetuating power hierarchies and imposing inappropriate and ineffective development approaches.

Despite these concerns, CSOs have become more central to global development agendas as major donors have become increasingly suspicious of state institutions as implementation partners. As a result, donors channel increasing amounts of global development funding through NGOs and CSOs to act either as service delivery partners for projects on health, water, education, and so on, or as agents in ensuring 'good governance' by the state through CSO and community-based monitoring of budgets, service delivery report cards, and other activities (Hammett and Jackson, 2021).

AS ONE CHAPTER ENDS…

So another will begin. This opening chapter has set up some of the big questions and ideas that frame global development, and that are addressed more detail in the rest of this book. The next chapter explores the shifting history of global development and the ideologies and ideals that have informed these agendas and policy frameworks. Throughout this history, the roles of key institutions and power brokers, and the language of and imagined geographies of development are prominent – from colonialism, through the birth of the 'modern' development era, to the MDGs and SDGs. While these recent goals have proven useful in providing a common language and influential framework for development agendas and popular mobilisation, extensive critiques remain – as we discuss next.

REFERENCES

Biccum, A. (2011). Marketing development: Celebrity politics and the "new" development advocacy. *Third World Quarterly*, 32 (7): 1331–1346.

Black, M. (2007). *The No-Nonsense Guide to International Development*. Oxford, UK: New Internationalist.

Brockington, D. (2002). *Fortress Conservation: The Preservation of the Mkomazi Game Reserve, Tanzania*. Bloomington: Indiana University Press.

Brundtland, G.H. (1987). Our common future—call for action. *Environmental Conservation*, 14 (4): 291–294.

Carmody, P. (2016). *The New Scramble for Africa*. Cambridge, UK: Polity Press.

Cornwall, A. (2007). Buzzwords and fuzzwords: Deconstructing development discourse. *Development in Practice*, 17 (4/5): 471–484.

Escobar, A. (1995). *Encountering Development: The Making and Unmaking of the Third World*. Princeton, NJ: Princeton University Press.

Escobar, A. (1999). The invention of development. *Current History*, 98 (631): 382–386.

Gates, B., Gates, M. (2014). Gates annual letter: 3 myths that block progress for the poor. Seattle, WA: Bill and Melinda Gates Foundation. http://www.gatesfoundation.org/Who-We-Are/Resources-and-Media/Annual-Letters-List/Annual-Letter-2014 (retrieved 15/12/2022).

Hammett, D. (2019). Whose development? Power and space in international development. *Geography*, 104 (1): 12–18.

Hammett, D., Jackson, L. (2021). The new age of the nation state? *Geography*, 106 (2): 76–84.

Horta, K. (2020). Paying the price for development. Bonn: D+C. https://www.dandc.eu/en/article/when-people-are-displaced-make-room-large-scale-development-projects-trauma-and (retrieved 14/12/2022).

IMF (2021). IMF executive directors and voting power. Washington, DC: IMF. https://www.imf.org/en/About/executive-board/eds-voting-power (retrieved 14/12/2022).

Khokhar, T., Serajuddin, U. (2015). Should we continue to use the term 'developing world'?, *TheDataBlog*. http://blogs.worldbank.org/openda ta/should-we-continue-use-term-developing-world (retrieved 15/12/2022).

Kothari, U. (2006). Critiquing "race" and racism in development discourse and practice. *Progress in Development Studies*, 6 (1): 1–7.

Liverman, D. (2018). Geographic perspectives on development goals: Constructive engagements and critical perspectives on the MDGs and the SDGs. *Dialogues in Human Geography*, 8 (2): 168–185.

Moyo, D. (2009). *Dead Aid: Why Aid is Not Working and How There is a Better Way for Africa*. New York: Macmillan.

Nielsen, L. (2011). Classification of countries based on their level of development: How it is done and how it could be done. IMF Working Paper WP/11/31.

Oxford English Dictionary (OED) Online (2023). development, n. Oxford: Oxford University Press. (retrieved 20/03/2023).

Peace Direct (2021). *Time to Decolonise Aid: Insights and Lessons from a Global Consultation*. London: Peace Direct.

Portes, A. (2012). Institutions and development: A conceptual reanalysis. In Portes, A., Smith, L. (eds) *Institutions Count: Their Role and Significance in Latin American Development* (pp. 1–23). Berkeley: University of California Press.

Portes, A., Smith, L. (2012). The comparative study of institutions: The 'institutional turn' in development studies. In Portes, A., Smith, L. (eds) *Institutions Count: Their Role and Significance in Latin American Development* (pp. 24–38). Berkeley: University of California Press.

Potter, R. (2001). Development and geography: 'Core and periphery'? *Area*, 33 (4): 422–427.

Rist, G. (2007). Development as a buzzword. *Development in Practice*, 17 (4/5): 485–491.

UN (1951). *Measures for the Economic Development of Underdeveloped Countries*. New York: Department of Social and Economic Affairs.

UN (1976). *Report of the World Conference of the International Women's Year, 19 June – 2 July 1975*. New York: UN. https://digitallibrary.un.org/record/586225?ln=en (retrieved 15/12/2022).

UNStats (2013). Composition of macro-geographical (continental) regions, geographical sub-regions and selected economic and other groupings. New York: UN Statistics Division. http://unstats.un.org/unsd/methods/m49/ (retrieved 07/12/2022).

Willis, K. (2014). Development: Geographical perspectives on a contested concept. *Geography*, 99 (2): 60–66.

2

DEVELOPMENT THROUGH THE AGES

Global development agendas are not neutral. They are framed not only by contemporary politics and ideology, but also the historical roles of colonialism, extractivism, empire, and exploitation. These histories contribute to current inequalities as well as dominant development policy and practice. The success of the industrial revolution in the UK, which underpins the country's current political and economic power, would not have been possible without the extraction of resources from her empire. The growth of plantation economies in the US and elsewhere would not have occurred without the horrors of the slave trade and exploitation of slave labour. Such recognition has led to arguments that aid should 'be understood as a form of systematic reparations for the violence inflicted' and for a move to talking of 'repair' rather than 'aid' (Peace Direct, 2021: 20).

Whether we talk of 'repair' or 'aid', the roots of global development pre-date US President Harry Truman's 1949 inauguration speech – which is commonly identified as launching the modern development era. Global development concerns can be traced back to the eighteenth century and the rise of imperialism. The entwining of economic growth and national development agendas was central to the practices of imperialism and colonialism. As explored in this chapter, advocates of imperialism maintained that overseas colonies provided opportunities to support economic development 'at home'. These ideological framings not only influenced colonial policy and practice at the time but have profound material (in terms of skewed infrastructural development) and psychological (in shaping how we think about global development) legacies that continue to the present day.

DOI: 10.4324/9781003155652-2

COLONIALISM

The era of colonialism underpins the contemporary global development landscape. Throughout this period, colonial powers sought to impose and intervene in the social, economic, political, and cultural structures of everyday life. The European experience – in terms of standards of living and political processes – was regarded as the optimum outcome, one to which all should aspire. As a result, early global development agendas were aligned with Enlightenment thinking and the view that European states, peoples, and ideas of rationality, progress, and modernity were not only superior, but that Europeans had a responsibility to 'uplift' the rest of the world to these standards. This narrative is often referred to as the 'white man's burden': an approach riddled with ideas of racial superiority and paternalism.

Colonial powers argued that subjugating local populations was necessary to promote development, maintain security, and promote economic growth. Justification for these interventions was often paternalistic, racist, and demeaning (Craggs, 2014), framed in narratives of a 'civilising mission' to 'uplift' and 'improve' populations who were perceived and represented as being 'backwards' or 'savage' and lacking in agency or ability to 'develop'. Thus, while colonial governments recognised that poverty existed in the colonies there was little interest or political will to tackle this. Rather, as Escobar (1995: 22) argues, the pervasive racism of colonialism meant that while colonial rulers believed some 'enlightenment' of the 'natives' was possible, economic development for 'natives' was pointless as, 'The natives' capacity for science and technology, the basis for economic progress, was seen as nil.'

This positioning of indigenous and local communities as primitive was also used to justify interventions that forcibly removed children from indigenous families and communities from their lands in various colonies around the world. These efforts were often supported through religious missionaries who played a powerful role in the 'civilising mission' of colonialism – initially through the promotion of Western (Christian) religion and conversion but evolving to encompass the provision of health and education facilities to local populations. These efforts, de facto, involved efforts to promote and instil Western values and behaviours.

However, rather than seeking to enhance living conditions in the colonies these efforts to promote modernisation and improve education, training, and health-care were less concerned with the quality of life of local populations than with legitimising colonialism and increasing economic productivity to support economic growth in the colonial power (Unger, 2018). These efforts were primarily about maintaining power and control over the colonies while ensuring resource extraction and profit maximisation to support the growth of the colonial power. As a result, efforts were made to impose 'modern' governance structures and replace or co-opt traditional power structures and hierarchies. Land was taken from communities and taxation systems introduced, forcing populations into new forms of work and labour relations. Infrastructural and other development projects were commissioned to support exports and other economic activities which would benefit the colonial power.

The development of infrastructure within the colonies was thus primarily aimed at supporting the extraction of profit and surplus to the colonial power while facilitating the projection of colonial rule and state power over territory and populations. As a result, there was little concern with or investment in supporting the internal or regional development of the colonies. The building of road and rail networks was instead designed to support the export of raw materials – as evidenced in the development of transport routes from the interior to major trading ports rather than between neighbouring states or within the colony. The legacies of these patterns of development – in terms of both physical infrastructure and also export-dependent economies – have lingered, presenting serious challenges to independent states.

The limited developmental benefits for colonies as a result of colonialism's extractive imperative meant that by the 1920s and 1930s colonial governments were facing increasing calls for more direct interventions to improve the standard of living of populations within the colonies (Unger, 2018). In part, these demands were mobilised by civil society organisations (CSOs) in response to humanitarian needs across Europe, Africa, and Latin America, meaning these organisations were at the forefront of early forms of humanitarian support. These pressures coincided with the introduction of Britain's 1929 Colonial Development Act and the French colonial loans project. These funding initiatives implemented grants for infrastructural projects in these powers' respective colonies. While presented as mechanisms to support improvements in quality of life within the colonies, in reality these projects asserted colonial power and control, and enhanced resource extractivism. By the 1940s growing pressures from colonial populations and CSOs forced colonial powers to establish funding mechanisms such as France's Fonds d'investissement pour le developpement economique et social in 1946 and Britain's Colonial Development and Welfare Act in 1940 to support social and economic development (Unger, 2018).

THE BIRTH OF THE 'MODERN' GLOBAL DEVELOPMENT ERA

The 1940s are seen as being the start of the 'modern' era of global development. Against the backdrop of World War II many of the dominant institutions of the contemporary global development industry emerged. The World Bank, IMF, and GATT were all established at the 1944 Bretton Woods conference, with the UN then following in 1949 with a mandate to promote global stability, growth, and development.

It was also the era of what is commonly viewed as the first major global development aid package – the Marshall Plan. Launched in 1948 by then-US Secretary of State George C. Marshall, the European Recovery Plan saw the US invest US$13 billion into rebuilding the war-ravaged economies of European and Scandinavian states including in the UK, France, Germany, Denmark, and others. Used to support the redevelopment of national infrastructures and stimulate economic growth, these funds were also key to American growth and prosperity. Europe was a key trading partner and it was in American interests to see European economies rebound in the post-war period as vital export destinations. Ultimately, the Marshall Plan was widely acclaimed as a success in facilitating post-war redevelopment and ensuring Western Europe remained a bulwark against Communist expansion.

As with colonial-era development agendas, the Marshall Plan was not an entirely altruistic development intervention. As noted earlier, this funding served American economic and geopolitical agendas, motivating factors that remained at the fore of global development policy and funding throughout the Cold War and beyond. Whether linked to efforts to build political support and alliances, or to gain preferential access to export markets or natural resources, bilateral global development funding was (and is) often framed by the donor's geopolitical or security agendas. For instance, the geopolitical and economic priorities of the US during the late 1940s and early 1950s are evident in the levels of economic support provided to Europe ($19 billion during 1945–1950, or over $3 billion per year on average) compared with the $150 million provided to the entirety of the global south in 1953 (Escobar, 1995: 33).

Against the geopolitical backdrop of the ideological Cold War between East and West, US President Harry S. Truman's (1949) inaugural speech is widely seen as the defining moment for the 'modern' development paradigm. Truman's speech positioned development at the heart of US (foreign) policy and set out a series of priorities and agendas to be tackled – including a focus on poverty and economic growth. His extolling of the merits of democracy (in contrast to the 'false philosophy' of Communism), and of American scientific and economic accomplishments, illustrates the politicised nature of his development agenda. Based on American 'pre-eminence', Truman set out a new vision for development in which the US would:

> embark on a bold new program for making the benefits of our scientific advances and industrial progress available for the improvement and growth of underdeveloped areas. More than half the people of the world are living in conditions approaching misery. Their food is inadequate. They are victims of disease. Their economic life is primitive and stagnant. Their poverty is a handicap and a threat both to them and to more prosperous areas. For the first time in history, humanity possesses the knowledge and skill to relieve suffering of these people. The United States is pre-eminent among nations in the development of industrial and scientific techniques ... I believe that we should make available to peace-loving peoples the benefits of our store of technical knowledge in order to help them realize their aspirations for a better life. And, in cooperation with other nations, we should foster capital investment in areas needing development ... It must be a worldwide effort for the achievement of peace, plenty, and freedom ... Such new economic developments must be devised and controlled to the benefit of the peoples of the areas in which they

are established ... The old imperialism – exploitation for foreign profit – has no place in our plans. What we envisage is a program of development based on the concepts of democratic fair-dealing ... Only by helping the least fortunate of its members to help themselves can the human family achieve the decent, satisfying life that is the right of all people.

(Truman, 1949)

In making this proclamation, Truman located the US as a beacon of aspiration and hope – an example for the world to follow. At the same time, he established a set of development priorities – poverty, hunger, disease, economic growth, democracy, and human rights – that continue to inform global development policy and practice today.

However, critics have argued that Truman's speech reflected and embedded a set of (neo-)colonial and imperial practices within development thinking and practice. The rhetoric of American pre-eminence and exceptionalism, and the desirability of 'the American dream of peace and abundance' provided a particular template as to what 'being developed' looked like and thus what should be aspired to (Escobar, 1995: 4). At the same time as promoting economic growth and technological advancement as *the* solution to development challenges, Truman's language created a geography of development: of the US (and the recovering economies of Europe) as being 'developed' and the global south as being 'underdeveloped' and in need of knowledge, expertise, and support from the US. Truman's speech therefore set out not only an economics-based approach to development, but also a rationale for Western interventionism which perpetuated assumptions of superiority, the 'white man's burden', and a neo-colonial relationship between the global north and south (Escobar, 1995; Hopper, 2018). These priorities and ideals dominated global development policy and funding during the 1950s.

1950s

Poverty and poverty reduction was the key focus of development agendas in the 1950s. According to dominant policy at the time, the solution to these challenges was economic growth and the accrual of material wealth. This focus on economic growth reflected the avowedly capitalist ideology of the US government and the Bretton Woods Institutions, and was used to justify calls for 'the total restructuring of "underdeveloped" societies' (Escobar, 1995: 4). The World Bank's decision to declare almost two-thirds of the world's population 'poor' (based on a unilateral decision to define countries with a per capita annual income of less than $100 as being poor) further fuelled this agenda. Crucially, as Escobar (1995) argues, the World Bank's 'discovering' and labelling of poverty as insufficient income not only identified the 'problem' but also predetermined the required solution – namely economic growth.

This mainstreaming of a capitalist economic policy agenda was dominant throughout the 1950s, evolving in relation to the shifting economic and geopolitical context. This context was framed by both the Cold War and the strengthening of anti-colonial movements and associated demands for independence and decolonisation. Consequently, global development agendas and funding flows were increasingly informed by colonial ties as well as geostrategic efforts to reinforce existing alliances and undermine rivals' coalitions.

Responding to the changing geopolitical landscape, major bilateral donors (such as the US) and multilateral funders (such as the Bretton Woods Institutions) began funnelling increasing amounts of development funding to states in the Middle East and Asia, and later Latin America and Africa to militate against the spread of Communism – particularly in newly independent states. The securitisation of development agendas at this time was clear in US policy and government agencies, through the role of the Mutual Security Agency (1951–1953) and Foreign Operations Administration (1953–1955) in directing US development spending in keeping with national security interests.

The polarisation of global politics during the 1950s not only informed the dominant global development terminology of the time (First, Second, Third Worlds), it also meant that much development aid and support were driven by Cold War politics. Newly independent states in the global south were viewed as potential allies by the Cold War superpowers, meaning vast sums of development aid (in the form of military support or equipment and financial payments) were expended in the pursuit of geostrategic interests with little regard for development outcomes.

Development policies were, in practice, often incorporated into or directed by foreign policy and national security agendas (Degnbol-Martinussen and Engberg-Pedersen, 2003).

This merging of security, economic, geopolitical, and development agendas means that the 1950s is often described as a period of developmentalist colonialism, or the second colonial occupation – this time focused upon developing colonies as trading partners. These processes involved investments from colonial powers to their colonies for infrastructural, educational, agricultural, and industry development. Presented as altruistic efforts to support the economic growth of the colonies, the primary goal of these investments was instead to protect the interests of the colonial power (Hopper, 2018). Central to the success of these efforts was the support of in-country elites and leaders. This resulted in an emphasis on providing either military support (to fight proxy wars and equip friendly governments) or top-down, technocratic infrastructure projects that offered little benefit for citizens but allowed elites to entrench their power. These large-scale projects were often intended both to promote industrialisation and to increase economic revenue and employment, while making symbolic statements to domestic and international audiences as to the technological prowess and realisation of 'modernity' of the state.

In summary, the development landscape of the 1950s was framed by and often subordinate to foreign policy and national security interests. Linked to the ideological agendas of the Cold War, Western donors prioritised market-led economic growth as *the* policy solution to realise poverty reduction and development outcomes. These priorities, and the continued dominance by global north institutions, meant development interventions were generally top-down and technocratic. This approach allowed for the cultivation of alliances with political elites, with populations reassured that the benefits of these grand development schemes would eventually 'trickle-down' to the poor.

1960s

The 1960s were designated as the UN *Decade of Development*. In adopting this decade-long strategic priority, the UN reaffirmed its commitment to 'promote social progress and better standards of life ... the advancement of the economic and social development of all peoples' (UN, 1961: 17), noting that development not only was seen as important to 'economically less developed countries ... but is also basic to the attainment of international peace and security' (UN, 1961: 17). Informing these sentiments, the UN resolution prioritised economic growth as the key solution to development challenges – setting a 5% per year national income growth target for all 'under-developed' countries. Reflecting the Keynesian economic ideology of the time (see chapter 4), this approach called for market-based solutions to promote and facilitate self-sustaining economic growth via industrialisation, diversification, and agricultural productivity, as well as state-backed measures to tackle education, hunger, and health.

The dominant approach to global development thus remained focused on economic growth, market-based approaches to poverty reduction, and top-down, infrastructure-heavy development projects with trickle-down economic benefits. Reflecting these priorities the Bretton Woods Institutions focused development support towards industrialisation and infrastructure projects including road, rail, water, sanitation, airports, ports, or energy projects. Overseas development remained a national priority for the US government, with US President John F. Kennedy pledging, in 1961, the 'best efforts' of the US to supporting 'those people in the huts and villages of half the globe struggling to break the bonds of mass misery' (Kennedy, 1961). US development agendas and funding were gradually reorientated towards Latin America, and the Peace Corps was established as a presidential initiative to support development in the global south through educational and technological support by American college-age volunteers.

While decolonisation continued apace (17 African countries declared independence from colonial rule in 1960), European development aid remained largely tied to colonial histories. In the first half of the decade, over 90% of bilateral aid spending by both France and the UK was provided to former colonies (Unger, 2018). At the same time, many newly independent states moved to adopt 'strong state' approaches to nation-building and national development projects, prioritising industrialisation-led development in an effort to rebalance national economies away from primary commodity resource-extraction (which left states highly

vulnerable to fluctuations in commodity prices). These development strategies resulted in huge demand for foreign investment
(including from the private sector), requests for preferential trade
deals with former colonial powers, as well as rapid increases in
demands for electricity – in turn resulting in major infrastructure
development projects to build hydroelectric dams and associated
infrastructure (Unger, 2018). At the same time, many newly independent states sought to renegotiate relations with former colonial
powers and challenge continued power hierarchies and attempts by
bi- and multi-lateral donors to impose universal (Western) development approaches and ideologies.

Global development policies at this time increasingly emphasised
the role of infrastructural and large-scale technological developments to underpin development as a longer-term process. Despite
the pace of decolonisation colonial-era ties and donors' geopolitical
and economic strategic self-interests dominated the global development landscape. As the *Decade for Development* ended the UN
lamented that global inequalities had increased and 'the level of
living of countless millions of people in the developing part of the
world is still pitifully low' (UN, 1970: 40).

1970s

Faced with growing global tensions and the failure of the first
Decade for Development to successfully achieve widespread poverty
reduction, the UN adopted the 1970s as a *Second Development
Decade*. This second decade set out to focus on global disarmament,
the elimination of colonialism, racial discrimination and apartheid,
and the promotion of equal rights for all. For the UN, the aim was
to 'bring about sustained improvement in the well-being of the
individual and bestow benefits on all. If undue privileges, extremes
of wealth and social injustices persist, then development fails in its
essential purpose' (UN, 1970: 40). To realise these ambitions, the
UN set out minimum annual economic growth rate targets for
countries in the global south, as well as strategies for increasing
employment, education enrolment, health programmes, nutrition,
and housing.

Despite the failure of economic-growth-led development agendas
during the 1960s, these same approaches dominated development

agendas in the 1970s, although greater attention to and strategies for addressing development in a more holistic manner became increasingly evident. The 'poor' remained the key focus to development agendas, and while market-led approaches still dominated poverty reduction efforts increased recognition emerged of the importance in promoting gender equality and social redistribution. This shifting engagement led to the emergence of integrated development approaches – linking education, health, welfare, sanitation, food, water, and other services to development outcomes. However, development projects remained generally conceived of at a large scale, with the delivery of these undermined by shortcomings in resources, staff availability, and other complications.

However, these efforts were hampered in the later part of the decade by the OPEC (Organisation of the Petroleum Exporting Countries) crisis. Also known as the 'energy crisis', this refers to the decision by key OPEC states to embargo the sale of oil to several leading economies (including the USA, UK, and Japan) in response to Western support for Israel in the Yom Kippur War. This led to oil prices soaring by nearly 300%, causing enormous economic disruption around the world. This crisis, coupled with rising inflation rates, further hindered the realisation of the goals of the *Second Development Decade* as increased costs meant that indebted poor states faced a perfect storm of increased debt servicing repayments, increased energy costs, and contracting markets for their products. These conditions laid the foundations for the 'lost decade' for development in the 1980s as a debt crisis engulfed many states in the global south.

1980s

Despite being designated as the UN's third *Decade for Development*, the aftermath of the OPEC crisis meant the 1980s came to be viewed as the 'lost decade' for development. Economic growth rates flatlined or fell amidst various debt crises and defaults around the world, with severe deterioration in economic conditions across Africa, Latin America, and Western Asia. Meanwhile, rising growth rates in China and South and East Asia resulted in growing divergence between regions. While other regions were subjected to the pressures of the neoliberal agenda to roll back the state, reduce state spending and taxation, and adopt a free-market approach for economic growth, state-led development approaches in China and parts of South and East Asia offered an alternative pathway to growth (see chapter 4).

The neoliberal shift in many major Western bilateral donor governments, with the election victories of neoliberal conservative politicians in the UK (Margaret Thatcher), USA (Ronald Reagan), and Germany (Helmut Kohl), had major impacts on global development agendas. The key ethos to this agenda was an unremitting focus on creating conditions for a free market (i.e. that goods and services could be traded within, across, and between national territories and economies with as few restrictions and limitations as possible). In practice this meant that governments were required to privatise state enterprises, reduce or remove protectionist policies on trade and investment, reform tax and public spending, and deregulate the business sector in order to receive development support.

This political and ideological shift amongst major donors was reflected in changes to development politics, resulting in even greater emphasis on privatisation and free-market-based economic growth as the primary solution to development needs. As a result, the tentative moves towards social redistribution made in the 1970s were reversed. New loans from the IMF and World Bank carried stringent pro-free-market conditionalities. Known as Structural Adjustment Programmes (SAPs), these required recipient governments to open domestic markets to free trade, strengthen governance structures, and reduce taxes and cut government spending on social services.

In essence, for countries to access loans and finance from the Bretton Woods Institutions, they had to surrender a degree of autonomy over decision making and commit to reducing taxes and public spending (typically realised through cuts to education, health, and social/welfare support budgets) and regulations of markets (which favoured global corporations at the expense of local businesses). This insistence on structural adjustments and opening of markets in the global south was not matched by the same reduction of protectionist policies in the global north, while overlooking the crucial historic role these policies played in helping countries in the global north develop their economies. Indeed, SAPs are now recognised as having had huge social and human costs, undermining human rights, and exacerbating poverty and deprivation for many – and, in particular, for women (Sadasivam, 1997; Mohan et al., 2000; and explored further in chapter 4).

Against the continued backdrop of the Cold War, the intersection of security and development also remained prominent. With continued large-scale investments in defence spending and military aid by major bilateral donors, the UN's Disarmament and Development Report (UN, 1987) argued for the moral case to shift government spending from armaments to meeting unmet social needs. Stating that world peace was jeopardised by the twin threats of over-armament and underdevelopment, the report cautioned that:

> The world can hardly be regarded as secure so long as there is polarisation of wealth and poverty at the national and international levels. Gross and systematic violations of human rights retard genuine socio-economic development and create tensions which contribute to instability. Mass poverty, illiteracy, disease, squalor and malnutrition afflicting a large proportion of the world's population often become the cause of social strain, tension and strife.
>
> (UN, 1987: 16–17)

These concerns, and the links drawn from poverty and deprivation to social tensions and conflict, have remained recurring concerns and narratives in relation to global development and the securitisation of development aid (Overton and Murray, 2021).

Meanwhile, the spread of television meant greater media coverage of major humanitarian crises, including the famine in Ethiopia between 1983 and 1985. This coverage contributed to increased public awareness of global development issues as well as new forms of celebrity humanitarianism and philanthropy. Perhaps the most iconic manifestation of this emergence was the Band Aid fundraising single *Do They Know It's Christmas?* and ensuing Live Aid concerts which raised over £150 million for aid projects in the Horn of Africa (Jones, 2017). The success of Band Aid, arising from the blend of celebrity, popular culture, vast media coverage, and feel-good altruism, was seen at the time as a fundamental rejection of Thatcherite ideology – but has come under increasingly critical scrutiny for promoting simplistic, colonial images of the global south (Jones, 2017; Müller, 2013; for further discussion on this, see chapters 6 and 7).

The 1980s also witnessed the mainstreaming of concerns with the environment and sustainability into development agendas, marked by the influential 1987 Brundtland Commission report. As Chair of the World Commission on Environment and Development, Norwegian Prime Minister Gro Harlem Brundtland (1987) called for action to ensure a common, sustainable future for humanity. Arguing that the world was at a crossroads due to our ability to alter planetary systems, Brundtland called attention to the threats posed by carbon dioxide emissions, the depletion of the ozone layer, desertification, acidification of soils and water, and deforestation. In the face of these fundamental threats to human security and survival Brundtland outlined the need to realise 'sustainable development' – which he understood as being continued economic growth but without environment damage and degradation. In making this case, Brundtland (1987: 292) stated that '[e]conomic growth is essential for sustainable development – for, without it, poverty will win against dignity and solidarity. Without growth we cannot create the capacity to solve environmental problems.'

Adopting a techno-optimist stance (i.e. that future technologies would facilitate economic growth without environmental damage), Brundtland argued that poverty was both a cause and a result of environmental degradation. The key drivers of both poverty and environmental damage were identified by Brundtland as being global political decisions and the limits to development options placed upon countries and communities in the global south by major donors and political powers in the global north. This report provided the first mainstreaming of sustainability and environmental concerns within Western development thinking and came amidst growing media coverage and popular awareness of global development concerns. These emergent themes would come increasingly to the fore during the 1990s.

1990s

Alongside growing concerns with sustainable development and a continued move away from 'top-down' to 'bottom-up' or 'grass-roots' development approaches, the fall of Communism and ending of the Cold War had major impacts on global development. The collapse of the Communist government in the USSR resulted in a rapid and major reduction in the country's role as a major development donor. For many client and recipient states, this resulted in major economic and social hardships as they suddenly lost access to development support, including heavily subsidised energy supplies, as well as the loss of a key trading partner and preferential market access. Simultaneously, the geopolitical and strategic priorities and interests of other major donors underwent rapid change, resulting in a delinking of development aid from foreign policy goals.

Other shifts were also occurring in the global development landscape. The Bretton Woods Institutions began to turn their attention to a 'good governance' agenda, with growing emphasis on and conditionalities linked to democratic practice. Parallel to these changes, there was a shift in rhetoric and policy towards 'development partnerships'. This policy turn saw a shift in donor priorities from shorter-term emergency relief towards longer-term humanitarian and development assistance, and a stronger (and belated) recognition of and role for aid recipients' agency, power, and knowledge. Changes in development agendas and thinking also shifted focus away from an economic-centric approach, instead recognising that poverty and development were multifaceted and required a more holistic approach.

At the same time, however, the acceleration of globalisation was widely viewed as a magic bullet for development, with increased trade and interconnectivity seen as being key to supporting economic growth in the global south. The rapid economic growth of the 'Asian Tiger' economies – Hong Kong, Singapore, South Korea, and Taiwan – was held up as both proof of concept and a blueprint for other countries to emulate. However, the Asian financial crisis of the late 1990s dispelled this vision, and the ensuing capital flight and debt crisis sent ripples through both the development sector and the global economy (national debt, the debt crisis, and the intensification of calls to 'drop the debt' are discussed in chapter 4).

THE 2000s: THE MILLENNIUM DEVELOPMENT GOALS

The turn of the millennium provided a symbolically powerful moment in relation to global development. Growing calls by development activists during the 1990s for donors to 'drop the debt' of heavily indebted poor countries (HIPCs) were prominent in many circles. At the same time, the UN mobilised global attention to development concerns through the launch of the Millennium Development Goals (MDGs). Aligned with this launch, the UN sought to emphasise the importance of collective mobilisation and global cooperation to realise a commitment to development as a humanist obligation. Before exploring the MDGs in more detail, it is important to note how these calls for global mobilisation on development issues were amplified but also complicated in the aftermath of the terrorist attacks on the US in September 2001. These attacks, known as the 9/11 attacks, had a profound and lasting impact on global relations and security agendas. With Western leaders responding to the attacks through the 'war on terror' there was also a revival of the 'securitisation of aid' agenda (Overton and Murray, 2021) and the linking of poverty to insecurity, instability, and terrorism. During this period, political leaders in the UK, US, and beyond spoke publicly of the link between uneven development, poverty, and radicalisation and generation of global terrorism (Potter, 2001). As a consequence, development funding and agendas shifted to focus on these concerns, including supporting the 'hearts and minds' campaign and post-conflict rebuilding efforts in Iraq, Afghanistan, and elsewhere.

The launch of the MDGs in September 2000 provided the first universal framework for global development, prefaced with the powerful statement that:

> As leaders we have a duty therefore to all the world's people, especially the most vulnerable and, in particular, the children of the world, to whom the future belongs [and ...] We are committed to making the right to development a reality for everyone and to freeing the entire human race from want.
>
> (UN, 2000: 1, 4)

In setting out this overarching framework, the UN hoped that the MDGs (Box 2.1) would provide a common cause for states to sign up to and commit overseas development aid spending towards. The provision of this framework – complete with specific goals and targets – was also seen as important in consolidating understandings of development as more than just economic growth. Instead, the range of goals emphasised a more holistic approach to global development that included consideration of the environment, health, education, and gender. The MDGs also provided a common language with which to talk about development, based around a set of 8 clear goals, 21 targets, and 60 indicators. This clarity in focus and language was a major success, helping to bring conversations around development into mainstream consciousness and conversation.

However, from the outset the MDGs were criticised for having been designed with very limited engagement and consultation, resulting in a top-down approach that legitimised and prioritised particular knowledges and political (neoliberal) ideologies (Hopper, 2018). This resulted in a continued emphasis on economic approaches to development – an approach exemplified in the MDGs talking of natural resources as being 'underutilised' and reducing their use-value to their potential economic value as extractive materials. This reductive approach failed to consider the environmental, social, and cultural value of these resources as well as the costs of their exploitation. This is a striking weakness to the MDGs, alongside a lack of attention to human rights (Hopper, 2018).

Further criticisms have argued that many of the stated goals were unrealistic and failed to consider local contexts (e.g. MDG 1.2 To achieve full and productive employment, as well as decent work for all, including young people and women) – be this in terms of economic resources, baseline starting points, or existing and likely future capacity. Thus, any hope of realising many of the goals relied heavily upon financial support from the global north: support that was not guaranteed and which became less viable in the aftermath of the 2008 financial crash which led many countries to reduce their ODA budgets.

BOX 2.1   THE MILLENNIUM DEVELOPMENT GOALS (MDGS)

1   Eradicate extreme poverty and hunger
2   Achieve universal primary education
3   Promote gender equality and empower women

4 Reduce child mortality
5 Improve maternal health
6 Combat HIV/AIDS, malaria and other diseases
7 Ensure environmental sustainability
8 Global partnership for development

The 2005 Paris Declaration of Aid Effectiveness sought to respond to some of these criticisms. This declaration emphasised the need for both more and more effective use of overseas development aid to achieve the MDGs, grounded in five key principles:

i ELDCs should own or lead development policies (i.e. recipients rather than donors should determine priorities and approaches).
ii International donors should support national development plans (rather than imposing their own agendas).
iii Donors should reduce costs to recipients through better coordination (rather than having multiple separate projects by different donors on a specific issue, donors should combine resources to support a single project with less duplication of bureaucracy and effort).
iv Both donors and recipients should commit to enhanced monitoring and evaluation of development projects (to identify any shortcomings or challenges and agree on responses to address and overcome them).
v There should be mutual accountability between donors and recipients for successes and shortcomings in outcomes (to reduce finger-pointing and encourage mutually beneficial outcomes).

Reviews of the Paris Declaration have been mixed, with critics noting that there were limited changes in donor practice in the following years and that too much energy and money were spent on bureaucracy rather than delivery. The means of defining and measuring 'effectiveness' have also been queried, while concerns have been raised of the failure to consider country contexts and the weaknesses in indicators for the five aims. Follow-up conferences in Accra (2008) and Busan (2011) sought to address various of these concerns, promoting transparency and accountability, sustainable development, reduction and elimination of 'tied aid', and a stronger role for global partnerships that includes new donors, civil society, and other funders.

For all these commitments and promises, how successful were we in realising the targets of the MDG era? In 2015, the UN Secretary General Ban Ki-Moon offered his thoughts on the successes and shortcomings of efforts towards these goals. Beginning with an upbeat tone, he stated:

> The global mobilization behind the Millennium Development Goals has produced the most successful anti-poverty movement in history. The landmark commitment entered into by world leaders in the year 2000 – 'to spare no effort to free our fellow men, women and children from the abject and dehumanizing conditions of extreme poverty' ... The MDGs helped to lift more than one billion people out of extreme poverty, to make inroads against hunger, to enable more girls to attend school than ever before and to protect our planet.
>
> (UN, 2015a: 3)

However, this was rapidly followed by a more sombre acceptance of continued inequalities and challenges in overcoming these:

> for all the remarkable gains, I am keenly aware that inequalities persist and that progress has been uneven. The world's poor remain overwhelmingly concentrated in some parts of the world. In 2011, nearly 60 per cent of the world's one billion extremely poor people lived in just five countries ... Progress tends to bypass women and those who are lowest on the economic ladder or are disadvantaged because of their age, disability or ethnicity ... further progress will require an unswerving political will, and collective, long-term effort.
>
> (UN, 2015a: 3)

Thus, while there was success in halving the numbers of people living in extreme poverty – from 1,926 million in 1990 to 836 million (or from 47% to 14% of those living in the global south) in 2015 – as well as other headline successes (Tables 2.1 and 2.2), many other goals were missed. At the same time dominant approaches to global development remained preoccupied with poverty alleviation, with limited attention to inequalities and disparities. Various of these were

Table 2.1 Indicative MDG outcomes – headline successes

MDG	Indicative outcome
1	Extreme poverty rate more than halved since 1990
2	Primary school enrolment in the global south up to 91%
3	Global equality in primary school enrolment for girls and boys realised
4	Under-5s mortality rate reduced by over half since 1990
5	Since 1990, maternal mortality ratio reduced by 45%
6	Millions of HIV infections and tuberculosis deaths averted
7	2.6 billion people gained access to improved drinking water since 1990
8	Aid spending had increased, reaching $135.2 billion in 2014

Table 2.2 UN MDG Report 2015 key outcomes (UN, 2015a)

MDG goal	Indicator	1990	2015
1	Extreme poverty rate	47%	14%
	Number living in extreme poverty	1,926 million	836 million
2	Primary school-age children out of school	100 million	57 million
3	Primary school enrolment ratio (girls/boys)	74: 100	103: 100
4	Global under-5s deaths	12.7 million	6 million
	Global under-5s mortality rate	90 per 1,000 live births	43 per 1,000 live births
	Global measles vaccination rate	73%	84%
5	Global maternal mortality ratio (deaths per 100,000 live births)	380	210
7	% using improved drinking water	76	91
	% urban population in slums in global south	39.4 (in 2000)	29.7 (in 2014)
8	ODA	$81 bn in 2000	$135 bn in 2014

acknowledged in *The Millennium Development Goals Report* (UN, 2015a), including concerns with significant gender inequalities, intra-national differences between the poorest and richest households, and between rural and urban areas as continuing development challenges. It was also recognised that millions still lived in poverty, hunger, and without reliable access to health, education, clean water, and sanitation.

Looking deeper into the data we see how global headlines can mask crucial regional and national variations. At the regional scale, the headline figures on poverty reduction (MDG 1 Eradicate extreme poverty and hunger) were dramatically skewed by the huge impact of China's economic growth. China's sustained economic growth, coupled with a large population, distorted the overall picture and contrasted with much slower changes in sub-Saharan Africa (see Table 2.3). We can see this when we look at the data.

Between 1990 and 2015:

- The global poverty rate dropped from 47% to 14% and the extreme poverty rate from 36% to 12%.
- In Eastern Asia, the extreme poverty rate dropped from 61% to 4% – driven by China's rapid economic growth.

Table 2.3 Percentages living on less than $1.25 per day (UN, 2015a)

	1990	*2011*	*2015*	*% decrease 1990–2015*
Sub-Saharan Africa	57	47	41	28
Southern Africa	52	23	17	66
Southern Asia (excl. India)	53	20	14	73
South-East Asia	46	12	7	84
China	61	6	4	94
Latin America and the Caribbean	13	5	4	66
Global south (excl. China)	41	22	18	57
All global south	47	18	14	69
World	36	15	12	68

- In Southern Asia, the extreme poverty rate dropped from 52% to 17%, influenced heavily by India's economic growth.
- In sub-Saharan Africa, there was no reduction in poverty rates between 1990 and 2002 before a decline in the 2000s – but over 40% of those living in sub-Saharan Africa remained in extreme poverty in 2015.

While we might commend China's economic growth and poverty reduction successes, what have been the costs of this growth? Has this growth been achieved at the expense of environmental damage (is it environmentally sustainable)? Have political, social, cultural, and human rights been realised or sacrificed in this process? Furthermore, can – or should – the conditions for China's economic growth be replicated elsewhere?

The continued persistence of poverty levels in other regions highlights the need for both more contextually specific policies and forms of support with poverty reduction *and* a more globally cooperative approach to tackling the structural factors which perpetuate global inequalities. One of the enduring weaknesses of both the MDGs and SDGs has been the failure to recognise and acknowledge the historical causes and factors of poverty and inequality. For some critics global development initiatives can only ever be at best a sticking-plaster or, worse, a conscience-salving distraction from the underlying historical and contemporary structural factors which underpin these inequalities. Thus, Diana Liverman (2018) has suggested that the focus on abstract goals and targets has dehumanised development, reducing it to a results-based management approach that is used to justify neoliberal capitalist-led development while ignoring systemic injustices, land dispossession, and the structural causes of poverty and hunger.

This results-based approach has also tended to focus on the national scale which, while useful for monitoring purposes and identifying regional variations and trends in realising the MDGs, hides intra-national differences and inequalities. A headline figure of national GDP growth may suggest success in reducing (extreme) poverty; but is this necessarily the case in reality? How is this increased income distributed? Are the poor benefitting from this increase? Are all regions benefiting – including across rural and urban spaces? In other words, to really understand the outcomes of development policies it is important to look at sub-national data, whether these are disaggregated (separated out) by gender, age, geographical location, or various other factors.

Why does this matter, you might ask? The simple answer is that development policies have differential impacts for different groups, and that priorities and needs will vary within a country. For example, access to drinking water, sanitation, or skilled health-care workers during childbirth can vary tremendously between rural and urban areas (Table 2.4). Alternatively, if measures of poverty reduction rely upon calculations of GDP per capita at a national scale it is impossible to consider how equitably any increase in GDP is realised across society. For instance, we know that SAPs had heavily gendered outcomes in agriculture as, typically, men took over the growing of cash-crops for export while women were forced onto more marginal land and the growing of sub-sistence crops (Sadasivam, 1997). It would be naïve to assume more recent development policies do not also have gendered impacts: Cornwall and Rivas (2015: 398) argue that the failure to include women's groups in the development of the MDGs has resulted in the negative outcome of 'making women work for development, rather than making development work for their equality and empowerment'. In other situations, economic growth may be heavily skewed to certain geographical regions within a country or concentrated amongst a particular social group or class (how some of these differences are measured and ranked is discussed in chapter 3). For instance, while South Africa's GDP per capita grew between 2006 and 2015 inequalities in poverty and income remained marked by racial, gender, and geographical factors: women earned 30% less then men, black Africans earned roughly

Table 2.4 Rural/urban comparison in access to health indicators, aggregated to a global level (UN, 2015a)

Indicator	Rural	Urban
% births attended by skilled health-care workers	56	87
% access to improved drinking water	84	96
% access to improved sanitation	50	72

28% of what their white counterparts did (R6,899 per month compared to R24,646 per month), while inequalities deepened in the Eastern Cape and Limpopo provinces (StatsSA, 2020).

Other questions also need to be asked about the data used to monitor the MDGs and development outcomes. First, what is the baseline for the data (i.e. the starting point for comparisons with outcomes)? Given the MDGs were launched in 2000, you might expect the baseline data to be from 2000 or perhaps 1999. And you'd be wrong. The baseline data used were from 1990! As Diana Liverman (2018) argues, this meant that the ambition of the MDGs was significantly weakened and success was almost guaranteed on many indicators given, for instance, that China's rapid economic growth during the 1990s then contributed to the post-2000 'success' against baseline targets.

Second, how targets are set and how 'progress' is measured are crucial. For instance, what would happen if the poverty indicator was moved from $1 per day to $1.25 per day, or even $2 per day? Or if it was adjusted to account for inflation? Over the lifetime of the MDGs, if inflation were at 2% per annum, the equivalent value of $1 in 2000 would be $1.35 in 2015. Liverman (2018: 173) makes this point, drawing on data from Pogge (2004) to demonstrate that when using a $1 per day threshold:

> poverty fell from 1481 million to 1092 million from 1981 to 2001, whereas at US$2 a day it increased by 285 m. In Sub-Saharan Africa, poverty at US$1.25 fell from 25% to 16% but at US$2.50 a day, poverty increased from 386 million to 610 million.

In other sectors, similar concerns were raised with the sustainability of outcomes – thus in relation to education goals a common question emerged along the lines of, 'education for all, for what?' Underpinning this question was not an opposition to increasing the percentage of children completing primary schooling, but a concern with: What happened after this? There wasn't the same level of expansion of secondary and tertiary education, nor were there necessarily clear policies to support employment creation. As a result, critics argued that targets became isolated, tick-box exercises which failed to support or promote more holistic national development agendas.

The MDGs were also critiqued for perpetuating the imagined geographies of global development which located it as happening 'over there'. Despite the official line that the MDGs were meant to apply to all countries, policies and practices were implemented in ways that meant 'it was the countries of the global south that were the targets of development action' (Willis, 2016: 107). This meant that the narrative and practice remained that the global north was 'developed' and played the role of benefactor to support the 'un/under-developed' global south, with very limited evidence of MDG-focused initiatives to support development *in* the global north. As the MDG era ended, the question was whether – or to what extent – the next iteration of development targets would learn from these critiques?

THE 2010s: THE SUSTAINABLE DEVELOPMENT GOALS

At the start of 2016, the MDGs were replaced by the SDGs. Setting the development agenda until 2030, the SDGs were widely celebrated as having been negotiated and agreed in a more inclusive and global process, and for positioning global development as being truly *global*. Introducing the SDGs, the UN's Agenda 2030 opens with the statement that it is a 'plan of action for people, planet and prosperity' (UN, 2015b: 3). At the heart of these ambitions is the eradication of 'poverty in all its forms and dimensions' with all members of the UN being 'resolved to free the human race from the tyranny of poverty and want and to heal and secure our planet … we pledge that no one will be left behind' (UN, 2015b: 3). Framing the overarching approach is a focus on three dimensions of sustainable development – economic, social, and environmental – with an emphasis (which clearly channels the spirit of the Brundtland Commission report (Brundtland, 1987)) on 'implement[ing] the Agenda for the full benefit of all, for today's generation and for future generations' (UN, 2015b: 7).

The 17 themes (Box 2.2) and 169 SDG targets apply to all countries. Take for instance SDG 1, End poverty in all its forms everywhere and target 1.2: 'By 2030, reduce at least by half the proportion of men, women and children of all ages living in poverty in all its dimensions according to national definitions.' This target goes beyond viewing the ending of poverty as being linked to the threshold of US$1.25 per day – which would keep the focus of ending poverty on the global south only – and challenges all governments to engage with development challenges, including but not limited to reducing poverty rates as measured against nationally defined thresholds. The SDGs can thus be understood as a more holistic and ambitious engagement with development, covering all countries, 'not just those who are seen as "deficient" in terms of income poverty, poor standards of living and high levels of maternal or child mortality' (Willis, 2016: 110).

BOX 2.2   THE 17 SUSTAINABLE DEVELOPMENT GOALS

The SDGs:

1   No poverty
2   Zero hunger
3   Good health and well-being
4   Quality education
5   Gender equality
6   Clean water and sanitation
7   Affordable and clean energy
8   Decent work and economic growth
9   Industry, innovation, and infrastructure
10 Reduced inequalities
11 Sustainable cities and communities
12 Responsible consumption and production
13 Climate action
14 Life below water
15 Life on land
16 Peace, justice, and strong institutions
17 Partnerships for the goals

As with the MDGs, the SDGs provide a clear and accessible common framework through which global development can be discussed and understood not only in academic or practitioner circles but also in political debate and popular conversation. As Grugel and Hammett (2016: 3) argue, 'The SDGs provide a template for demanding more intensive, focussed action by governments and civil society to tackle some of the pressing challenges around global inequalities and to hold power-holders to account.' This template, however, is not cheap. Even prior to the Covid pandemic (which has exacerbated many inequalities and development challenges) it was estimated that the costs of realising the SDGs would amount to US$2–3 trillion per year, or 4% of global GDP. This cost is far in excess of the current 0.7% of GDP target for countries in the global north to commit to overseas development aid (Overton and Murray, 2021: 3).

Progress towards meeting the SDGs was already mixed prior to the Covid pandemic – a global crisis which has obliterated four years of progress in reducing poverty rates and undermined progress on multiple other goals. Add in the impacts of the increasing frequency and intensity of extreme weather events due to climate change, the war in Ukraine – in terms of rising inflation and fuel costs, disruptions to global food supplies, etc. – and the costs of meeting the SDGs are escalating. These mixed outcomes are reflected in varying progress on SDG targets at both global and regional levels. The UN's 2022 SDG progress report illustrates this succinctly, highlighting stalled progress on eradicating extreme poverty at a global scale and growing levels of extreme poverty in North Africa and West Asia, and Latin America and the Caribbean. Negative trends or stalled progress are also reported across targets to reduce proportions of unsentenced detainees, prevent extinction of threatened species, ensure conservation and sustainable ecosystem usage, increase biodiversity protection, reduce greenhouse gas emissions, and achieve full employment. On the flip side, near-universal positive progress is reported on increasing the coverage of births attended by skilled health personnel, achieving universal access to electricity, increased access to mobile networks, and increased internet use. (You can find really informative and helpful infographics and visuals on progress towards meeting the SDGs at https://unstats.un.org/sdgs/rep ort/2022/progress-chart/; https://unstats.un.org/sdgs/report/2022/; https://unstats.un.org/sdgs/report/2022/SDG_report_2022_infograp hics.pdf; and https://odi.org/en/publications/projecting-progress-rea ching-the-sdgs-by-2030/.)

However, the SDGs are far from perfect. Critics have argued that while the SDGs place emphasis on the environment, social development, and inclusive and sustained economic growth, they fail to address major underlying structural issues including the current dominant neoliberal economic order (McCloskey, 2015). Groups such as Global Justice Now (previously the World Development Movement) have argued that the SDGs are not radical enough and allow for business-as-usual in global inequalities in power, wealth, and justice (Grugel and Hammett, 2016). Equally, while the development of the SDGs was informed by greater discussion of gender, issues of women's empowerment and gender equality either fall away in practice or are reduced to descriptive categories rather than substantive concerns (Cornwall and Rivas, 2015).

A second major challenge – and one returned to in chapter 5 – is the continued ways in which global development is talked about. The SDGs are cast as being globally relevant – so that the goals apply as much to the UK, Canada, or Belgium as much as they do to Lesotho, Laos, or Argentina. However, when was the last time a British politician spoke of the need for policy or funding to meet the SDGs in the UK? Have you ever read in a newspaper or overheard someone on the radio or television talking about the SDGs in relation to a country in the global north? Despite efforts to position the SDGs as a global endeavour, the everyday political and popular understanding and narrative remain that they apply 'out there' and are only relevant to the global south.

Other criticisms include the SDGs containing too many goals (and many of them are vague and/or unrealistic), that indigenous communities have been marginalised, and that national debt is poorly considered (Hopper, 2018). Compounding these concerns, an emphasis on free trade remains without efforts towards a redistributive agenda. While the focus may be on helping the bottom 40%, there are no calls for progressive efforts to redistribute wealth and resources from the top 1%. Linked to this, and given increased urgency by the climate crisis, there are profound contradictions between goals – not least between goals for environmental sustainability and a continued emphasis on economic growth.

The UN is not oblivious of these challenges, and the annual Global Sustainable Development reports can make for sobering reading. For instance, the 2019 report states, bluntly, that 'the world is not on track for achieving most of the 169 targets' (UN, 2019: xx) and – more concerningly – that things are going backwards in key areas relating to the SDGs including rising inequalities, increasing challenges from climate change, continued biodiversity loss, and waste from human activities. The report also notes that extreme poverty continues to be concentrated among marginalised groups and that inequalities are perpetuated by vicious circles including links between a lack of access to education, higher rates of unemployment, lower income, a lack of social protection, increased vulnerabilities to hunger, lack of access to health-care, and lack of power in household decision-making.

Channelling the spirit of Brundtland (1987) again, the 2019 report expresses concern that 'no country is yet convincingly able to meet a set of basic human needs at a globally sustainable level of resource use' (UN, 2019: xx). The argument is made, however, that science and technology will provide solutions which will allow the continued pursuit of increasing levels of human well-being and economic growth while maintaining a healthy environment. However, critics have dismissed this view, arguing that there is no compelling evidence that science and technology will be able to provide such solutions and our focus instead should be upon addressing and mitigating these challenges now, rather than deferring them to some unspecified point in the future.

IN SUMMARY

This chapter has illustrated not only how notions of and approaches to global development have evolved over time, but also that the concept and idea of 'development' remain highly contested and politicised. Who defines what development is, where it should happen and to whom, what the priorities are, and how development is measured all remain powerful questions and considerations. Further complicating the picture are questions of global economic orthodoxy, environmental sustainability, geopolitical agendas, and the seemingly inevitable entwining of national self-interest with global development engagements.

REFERENCES

Brundtland, G.H. (1987). Our common future—call for action. *Environmental Conservation*, 14 (4): 291–294.

Cornwall, A., Rivas, A.-M. (2015). From 'gender equality and 'women's empowerment' to global justice: Reclaiming a transformative agenda for gender and development. *Third World Quarterly*, 36 (2): 396–415.

Craggs, R. (2014). Development in a global-historical context. In Desai, V., Potter, R. (eds) *The Companion to Development Studies* (pp. 27–31). Abingdon: Routledge.

Degnbol-Martinussen, J., Engberg-Pedersen, P. (2003). *Aid: Understanding International Development Cooperation*. London: Zed Books.

Escobar, A. (1995). *Encountering Development: The Making and Unmaking of the Third World*. Princeton, NJ: Princeton University Press.

Grugel, J., Hammett, D. (2016). Introduction: A call for action in a multi-disciplinary world. In Grugel, J., Hammett, D. (eds) *The Palgrave Handbook of International Development* (pp. 1–18). London: Palgrave.

Hopper, P. (2018). *Understanding Development*. 2nd ed. Cambridge, UK: Polity Press.

Jones, A. (2017). Band Aid revisited: Humanitarianism, consumption and philanthropy in the 1980s. *Contemporary British History*, 31 (2): 189–209.

Kennedy, J.F. (1961). Inaugural address, January 20, 1961. Boston, MA: John F. Kennedy Presidential Library and Museum; National Archives and Records Administration. https://www.jfklibrary.org/archives/other-resources/john-f-kennedy-speeches/inaugural-address-19610120 (retrieved 21/03/2023).

Liverman, D. (2018). Geographic perspectives on development goals: Constructive engagements and critical perspectives on the MDGs and the SDGs. *Dialogues in Human Geography*, 8 (2): 168–185.

McCloskey, S. (2015). From MDGs to SDGs: We need a critical awakening to succeed. *Policy & Practice: A Development Education Review*, (20): 186–194.

Mohan, G., Zack-Williams, A.B., Brown, E., Milward, B., Bush, R. (eds) (2000). *Structural Adjustment: Theory, Practice and Impacts*. Hove: Psychology Press.

Müller, T. (2013). The long shadow of Band Aid humanitarianism: Revisiting the dynamics between famine and celebrity. *Third World Quarterly*, 34 (3): 470–484.

Overton, J., Murray, W. (2021). *Aid and Development*. Abingdon: Routledge.

Peace Direct (2021). *Time to Decolonise Aid: Insights and Lessons from a Global Consultation*. London: Peace Direct.

Pogge, T. (2004). The First United Nations Millennium Development Goal: A cause for celebration? *Journal of Human Development*, 5 (3): 377–397.

Potter, R. (2001). Development and geography: 'Core and periphery'? *Area*, 33 (4): 422–427.

Sadasivam, B. (1997). The impact of structural adjustment on women: A governance and human rights agenda. *Human Rights Quarterly*, 19 (3): 630–665.

StatsSA (2020). How unequal is South Africa?Pretoria: Statistics South Africa. https://www.statssa.gov.za/?p=12930 (retrieved 03/01/2023).

Truman, H. (1949). Inaugural address. Independence, MO: Harry S. Truman Library & Museum. https://www.trumanlibrary.gov/library/public-papers/19/inaugural-address (retrieved 15/12/2022).

UN (1961). *17 10(XVI) United Nations Development Decade Resolution* (pp. 17–18). New York: United Nations.

UN (1970). *2626 (XXV) International Development Strategy for the Second United Nations Development Decade* (pp. 40–49). New York: United Nations.

UN (1987). *Report of the International Conference on the Relationship between Disarmament and Development, New York, 24 August-11 September 1987.* New York: United Nations.

UN (2000). *A/RES/55/2. United Nations Millennium Declaration.* New York: United Nations. https://www.un.org/en/development/desa/population/migration/generalassembly/docs/globalcompact/A_RES_55_2.pdf (retrieved 14/03/2023).

UN (2015a). *The Millennium Development Goals Report.* New York: United Nations.

UN (2015b). *A/RES/70/1. Transforming Our World: The 2030 Agenda for Sustainable Development.* New York: United Nations.

UN (2019). *The Future is Now: Science for Achieving Sustainable Development – Global Sustainable Development Report 2019.* New York: United Nations.

Unger, C. (2018). *International Development: A Postwar History.* London: Bloomsbury Academic.

Willis, K. (2016). International development planning and the Sustainable Development Goals (SDGs). *International Development Planning Review,* 38 (2): 105–111.

3

UNDERSTANDING AND MEASURING DEVELOPMENT

As our understandings of global development have shifted, so too have the ways in which development is defined and measured. Economics-based approaches have generally held sway over Western attitudes to development – however, these approaches have increasingly been challenged by moves towards more holistic understandings. At the same time, there has been growing sensitivity to 'alternative' and indigenous understandings of development, many of which pre-date dominant Western approaches.

Infusing the debates outlined in this chapter are differing agendas and ideologies which, in turn, produce different sets of priorities and measures for development. At the crux of the tensions between different approaches to and theories of development are differing beliefs as to not only what 'development' is but also what is 'worthwhile' development, and what can be learnt from experiences when development agendas produce negative or bad outcomes.

DEVELOPMENT AS ECONOMIC GROWTH

Mainstream global development policies and donors continue to focus on economic growth (driven by industrialisation) as the primary route to poverty reduction and the realisation of development goals. This approach is evident in the work of influential figures including Paul Collier and Jeffrey Sachs. Drawing on Keynesian economics, Collier (2008) argues we should be less worried about the *type* of economic growth than about the absolute level

DOI: 10.4324/9781003155652-3

or *amount* of growth. His argument is, in essence, that high levels of economic growth will de facto drive poverty reduction and development and he points to the slow economic growth rate of the poorest countries as evidence for this. Meanwhile, Jeffrey Sachs' (2005) influential 'differential diagnosis' argument was premised upon a belief that net capital accumulation needs to exceed population growth to realise poverty reduction. Sachs' approach focused on six types of capital (human, business, infrastructure, natural, public institutional, and knowledge) as vital to economic growth, while also considering the dynamics of poverty (and poverty reduction) at both household and national levels.

Linked to this privileging of economic growth as the golden bullet for development, we commonly see global development discussion framed in terms of economic measures such as a country's Gross Domestic Product (GDP), Gross National Product (GNP), and variations upon these. These data are commonly used not only to measure economic growth and development, but also to define and characterise the developmental level and needs of countries. Hence, governments, multilateral organisations, and donors have often used economic indicators to identify countries as belonging to specific development categories. As a result, we hear countries being described as less or more economically developed, or as low-, lower-middle-, upper-middle-, or high-income based upon their GDP or GNP per capita.

What is a country's GDP? Put simply, this is the total value of all goods and services produced within the country. GNP meanwhile is the total value of all goods and services claimed as being produced by residents within the country – so, a country can 'claim' profits generated abroad but then lose the income claimed by other countries. These figures can then be divided by the population of the country to provide a per capita indicator.

You might be thinking, why not just use the total value produced by a country as the indicator? At times, we do hear discussion of which countries have the largest economies – and thus the most economic power. However, simply looking at the overall size of an economy overlooks the population – and this is where the 'per capita' aspect becomes important. Let's take as a simple example China and the US. In 2020, these were the two biggest economies in the world: the US had a GDP of $21 billion, China

$15 billion. However, on a per-capita basis, the US ranked eighth wealthiest in the world ($63,206 per capita) while China ($10,434 per capita) ranked 63rd. For the sake of comparison, the highest-ranked country for GDP per capita in 2020 was Monaco ($173,688), and the lowest was Burundi ($239).

GDP per capita remains a commonly used and understood measure as it can be used both to define and highlight economic inequalities between countries or regions – for instance between 'high-income' and 'low-income' states, or between North America and Eastern and Southern Africa (see Tables 3.1 and 3.2). Despite its common usage, GDP per capita is a crude and problematic development indicator. Not only does it fail to consider other markers of development (as we shall explore) but as a national-level figure it masks internal inequalities in income levels (i.e. the differences between the richest and poorest within a country) and is unable to account for the local cost of living.

Responding to the cost of living concern, we see the use of GDP Purchasing Power Parity (GDP PPP). This approach adjusts the dollar-value of GDP per capita to reflect the cost of goods – including items such as bread, milk, furniture, fuel, etc. – in each country. In states where goods are more expensive, the purchasing power of their GDP is reduced compared to those countries where goods cost less. In other words, GDP PPP allows us to understand how much money is needed in each country to purchase the same

Table 3.1 GDP per capita in US$ (2020) by World Bank development definition

Development category	GDP per capita (US$)
High-income	43,934.55
World	10,916.08
Upper-middle-income	9,177.89
Middle-income	5,216.97
Lower-middle-income	2,217.22
Least developed countries: UN classification	1,053.23
Heavily indebted poor countries (HIPCs)	968.69
Low-income	691.17

Table 3.2 GDP per capita in US$ (2020) by global region

Region	GDP per capita (US$)
North America	61,161.15
European Union	34,173.49
Europe & Central Asia	23,963.34
East Asia & Pacific	11,477.49
World	10,916.08
Latin America & Caribbean	7,243.67
Middle East & North Africa	6,534.56
South Asia	1,823.71
Sub-Saharan Africa	1,501.15

'basket' of goods and this is used to adjust GDP data to reflect the cost of living. A more light-hearted version of this has been *The Economist*'s 'Big Mac Index' – based on the assumption that a Big Mac is the same everywhere, this measure uses the price of a Big Mac in different countries as a proxy for the cost of living and thus provides a very informal measure of purchasing power parity (other variations also exist, including the KFC index).

Why is this important? Simply put, income that may put you on the poverty line in one country could lift you well above the poverty line in a second or plunge you deep into poverty in another depending on the relative cost of living. Again, however, this approach is unable to give insights into economic inequalities within a country. While Collier may argue this is unimportant (remember, for Collier it is the amount rather than distribution of economic growth that matters), in reality it is vital to understand how and where economic growth is occurring.

Identifying sub-national inequalities is crucial for global development: headline economic growth may look positive, but if this wealth and income is disproportionately benefiting the already-rich this does little to realise development goals and may instead fuel social tensions and divisions. For instance, Tanzania's economy grew on average by 4% each year between 1990 and 2000, but the number of people in poverty grew by 3%. Meanwhile, Angola's economy has grown dramatically on the back of the extractive oil industry, but these profits have benefited a small in-country elite and international investors rather than the majority of citizens. More broadly, these GDP-based indicators not only struggle to account for inequalities *within* a state, but also cannot account for or measure well-being, quality of life, access to education or health-care, or life expectancy. The focus on GDP as a marker of development has resulted in economic growth becoming an end unto itself, rather than as an end to realise sustainable development. Crucially, this dominant approach often fuels inequalities (as explored later), while failing to account for the negative externalities generated by economic growth. Negative externalities are the costs or 'ills' that arise from a process or activity and which are experienced elsewhere – for instance, greenhouse gas emissions from industrialisation in one country have environmental and economic costs that affect many countries. At present, these external (and future) costs remain unaccounted for, incurring no direct costs to the producer or emitter.

DEVELOPMENT AND POVERTY REDUCTION

Economics-centred approaches to development have prioritised poverty reduction as a development outcome. But what is poverty, and how is it measured? Put simply, poverty is a deprivation of well-being. Traditionally, poverty has been measured in simple economic terms: at the start of the twenty-first century, the World Bank defined the International Poverty Line as $1 per day GDP PPP, updating this to $1.25 in 2008, $1.90 in 2015, and then $2.15 in 2022 to reflect increases in the cost of living.

Such a relatively simple approach provides a clear and accessible way of talking about poverty for both political and popular discussion – and can be linked to measurable targets. For instance, linked to MDG 1 *Eradicate extreme poverty and hunger*, we saw the target 'To halve the proportion of people whose daily income is less than $1.25'. Currently, SDG 1 *No poverty* includes the target to 'eradicate extreme poverty for all people everywhere, currently measured as people living on less than $1.25 a day'. Talking about levels of poverty (as a proxy for development) can provide a seemingly simple and accessible snapshot. Take for example, the headline figures that in 1820 94% of households globally were living in poverty, a figure that dropped to 82% in 1900 and which has continued to fall (Jefferson, 2020). Sounds positive, doesn't it? But what happens when we look at the actual *number* of households in poverty? This has gone up, as the global population has increased, so that in 2015 there were 736 million people living in extreme poverty, with a further 1 billion living on between $2 and $3 per day and therefore highly vulnerable to slipping into extreme poverty (Jefferson, 2020; UN, 2019: xxiii). UN Women (2022) develop these ideas further, alongside efforts to estimate the gendered nature of (extreme) poverty – 388 million women and girls lived in extreme poverty in 2022, compared with 372 million men and boys, with the majority of these women and girls (244 million) living in sub-Saharan Africa – they illustrate how relatively small changes in the International Poverty Line would result in massive changes to poverty rates (Table 3.3).

Returning to SDG 1, we see growing recognition that the International Poverty Line is unable to account for national context: 'to reduce at least by half the proportion of men, women and

Table 3.3 Changing poverty rates using different poverty line values (UN Women, 2022)

Region/poverty line	$1.90	$3.20	$5.50	National
Australia & New Zealand	0.3	0.5	0.7	12.2
North America and Europe	0.5	0.9	2.2	14.0
Eastern and South-Eastern Asia	1.6	7.4	21.1	7.3
Latin America and the Caribbean	6.0	12.7	27.9	30.4
Western Asia and North Africa	7.4	19.0	41.4	22.6
Central and Southern Asia	8.1	36.7	71.4	20.7
Oceania (excl. Australia & New Zealand)	21.7	44.9	72.5	34.3
Sub-Saharan Africa	42.3	68.3	86.7	41.2

children of all ages living in poverty in all its dimensions according to *national definitions*' (emphasis added). This wording indicates an awareness that the International Poverty Line is relatively unhelpful in some countries, but that these countries still have significant proportions of their populations living in poverty compared to national living costs. In addition, the wording also alludes to an understanding of poverty as more than just income – and not simple in terms of differential outgoings and fixed costs, or realisable assets or savings that individuals or households may have. The mention of 'all its dimensions' signals an attempt to move beyond relatively blunt economic measures and towards a more holistic view of poverty.

Before we move to consider more holistic and multidimensional approaches to poverty, it is important to think about some of the language used around poverty – such as relative, absolute, extreme, and moderate poverty. What do these terms mean?

Extreme or absolute poverty refers to households that are unable to meet basic survival needs and lack access to fundamental necessities such as adequate food, clean water, shelter, basic medicines, and the like (Hussain, 2020). This group would include Paul Collier's *Bottom Billion* or can be understood using Jeffrey Sachs' thinking as being those unable to get onto the first rung of the development ladder. These are households that are struggling to survive on a day-to-day basis and would fall below the International Poverty Line. Crucially, and signalling a broader definition of poverty than pure economics, the UN's definition of absolute poverty – adopted at the 1995 Copenhagen World Summit on Social Development – includes *both* income and access to services. Thus, for the UN, absolute poverty is understood as 'a condition characterised by severe deprivation of basic human needs, including food, safe drinking water, sanitation facilities, health, shelter, education and information. It depends not only on income but also on access to services' (UN, 1995: 57). Layered onto this definition, the UN identifies overall poverty as also including increased morbidity and mortality, social discrimination, and exclusion from or lack of participation in civic and social life (UN, 1995).

Moderate poverty is commonly used to refer to households whose basic needs are just barely met, but who remain vulnerable to illness or other crises wiping out savings and income. Such households are likely to be in long-term conditions of chronic poverty (in other words, remaining poor for very long periods of time or entire lifetimes), with limited ability to accrue the resources needed to move out of poverty.

Relative poverty can refer to those with a household income below a specific proportion of national average income or can be a more subjective measure based upon ability to access those things that are seen as 'essential'. Thus, if the British government's own poverty line definition of a household living on less than 60% median income is used, the Child Poverty Action Group (CPAG) estimates that 14 million people in the UK are living in poverty. The Social Metrics Commission, which uses the same baseline but incorporates both major outgoings (housing costs, childcare costs) and accessible savings into calculations, places this figure at 16.6 million. There are various other alternative approaches to think about hardship within specific national contexts – for instance, in the UK CPAG goes on to estimate that 100,000 children lack three meals a day or do not own a warm winter coat, while 3.2 million children don't have a one-week holiday in a year.

Thinking about hardship (an inability to pay for essentials) and social exclusion in relation to poverty provides an alternative and more multifaceted approach. The question emerges then as to: What is essential and who determines this? Are essentials simply access to basic nutrition, shelter, and health-care? Or does this include access to hot water, clean clothes, a television, or being able to afford a holiday? In the UK, the Joseph Rowntree Foundation's poverty measure is based on popular perceptions of adult and child necessities – including being able to eat fresh fruit and vegetables every day, living in a damp-free house, being able to afford festive celebrations, and having a bed to sleep in (Gordon et al., 2000).

Chronic poverty refers to those who are always or usually below the poverty line and is most commonly faced by those experiencing multiple forms of discrimination based on caste, gender, immigrant, religious identity, disability, or other characteristics. Chronic poverty is often also intergenerational – growing up poor often limits access to and outcomes from education, health services, employment, and life opportunities. Other structural factors can also have an important role here – consider for example the chronic poverty experienced by indigenous communities in Bolivia. A combination of remoteness from major urban areas, high travel costs, limited access to education and health-care, stigmatisation, and barriers faced in registering for government services meant indigenous communities were often marginalised from political, social, and economic rights and opportunities (Hulme, 2003).

The *transitory or churning poor* refers to those who frequently move in and out of poverty, who are unable to sustain savings and are thus vulnerable to unexpected crises (medical bills, crop failure, and similar).

In recent years, measures and understandings of poverty have expanded beyond simply income and economics. Golding and Reinert (2012) use income, health, education, empowerment, and working conditions as measures of poverty. Approaches such as the Multidimensional Poverty Indicator (MPI; developed by the Oxford Poverty and Human Development Initiative (OPHI)) are increasingly based on how poverty is experienced and include indicators covering income and savings, but also levels of education, health-care, environmental quality, and political freedoms (Alkire and Sumner, 2013). Using ten different indicators of poverty (Table 3.4), the MPI provides insights into not only *who* is poor but *how* they are poor and how poverty is distributed and

Table 3.4 Components and weightings of the OPHI Multidimensional Poverty Indicator

Dimension of poverty	Indicator	Weighting
Health	Nutrition	1/6
	Child mortality	1/6
Education	Years of schooling	1/6
	School attendance	1/6
Living Standards	Cooking fuel	1/18
	Sanitation	1/18
	Drinking water	1/18
	Electricity	1/18
	Housing	1/18
	Assets	1/18

encountered across different regions and communities within a country (OPHI, 2021).

POVERTY OR INEQUALITY?

While poverty reduction remains the key development policy focus, there are growing calls to look beyond economic growth and numbers living in poverty and to pay greater attention to inequalities. Simply looking at national income levels reveals little about inequalities: both wealthy and poorer nations can be highly unequal (e.g. the US, India) or can be relatively equal (e.g. Norway, Uruguay). Inequalities in income and wealth are perhaps the most commonly discussed – and eye-wateringly stark: the 2022 *World Inequality Report* (Chancel et al., 2022) highlights that the top 0.1% of the world's population own 11% of wealth, the top 1% own 38% of total wealth, while the bottom 50% own just 2%. A similar pattern is evident for income: the richest 10% benefit from 52% of income, the poorest 50% get 8.5% (Chancel et al., 2022). But this focus on income – or on wealth – offers a very partial view of inequalities.

Inequalities are, in simple terms, the differences in access to resources and opportunities – be this income, education, health services, voting rights, and so on. Understanding inequalities is crucial within global development, due to not only the risks of increasing inequalities leading to social instability and unrest, but also the need to address the intersectionalities of inequality. When we talk of intersectionalities, we are referring to the multiple factors which affect or are experienced by an individual (for instance due to characteristics including gender, age, ethnicity, religion, and so on) which can reinforce their marginalisation or privilege.

Inequalities must therefore be considered in terms of both opportunities (who can access what opportunities based upon personal background and identity markers, discrimination) and outcomes (levels of income or educational outcomes, exposures to harmful environments). Inequalities in opportunities and outcomes are, to a large extent, self-sustaining – being born into privilege provides more opportunities for a fulfilling life, whereas being born into disadvantage means fewer such opportunities. Crucially, then, inequalities are often intergenerational, limiting not only the life chances of one generation but also the following generations.

Economic, political, social, and spatial inequalities often co-occur and can result in self-perpetuating cycles of advantage and disadvantage. We see this process occurring across the globe in relation to gender pay gaps, the spatial marginalisation of social and informal housing to urban peripheries, differential class-based educational and health outcomes, and so on.

Although reducing inequalities – both within and between countries – is a core commitment of SDG 10, the related targets only address poverty alleviation rather than wealth and income distribution (Fukuda-Parr, 2019). More widely, debates continue over what level of inequality is 'good' or 'acceptable' – with some arguing that inequalities drive aspirations and achievement, while others argue inequalities are divisive, self-perpetuating, and risk fuelling social tensions. As a result, despite the combined wealth of the richest 1% of the world growing from 27% of total wealth in the 1980s to 33% in 2017 – and the poorest 75% holding around 10% of total wealth – efforts towards a progressive redistribution of wealth to support global development agendas remain negligible (UN, 2019: 16). Instead, policies of deregulation and liberalisation continue to fuel the rise in inequalities meaning 'inequality is not inevitable, it is a political choice' (Chancel et al., 2022: 11).

In all of these discussions, scale matters – measures of inequality at the global scale are useful, but so are those at national or subnational levels. In 2021, the top 10% in the MENA region secured 58% of income, with the top 10% in Latin America and Sub-Saharan Africa also securing at least 55% of income, while the bottom 50% captured less than 10% of income (Chancel et al., 2022). At the national scale common measures of inequality include the GINI coefficient and the Palma Ratio.

The GINI coefficient is a statistical approach that measures the (in)equality of income distribution within a country, with a score of 0 indicating perfect equality (all residents have the same income) through to a score of 1 indicating absolute inequality (one person has all the country's income to themselves, and everyone else has nothing). Commonly, countries with a score of between 0.2 and 0.35 are seen as relatively equitable, whereas those with scores over 0.5 are seen as highly unequal. The GINI index, used by the UNDP, is based on the same principles and scores countries between 0 and 100 with higher scores again indicating greater levels of inequality. We thus see South Africa (63.0), Namibia (59.1), Zambia (57.1), and Colombia (54.2) as amongst the most inequitable, and the Slovak Republic (23.2), Belarus (24.4), Slovenia (24.4), and the United Arab Emirates (26.0) amongst the most equitable. The two richest countries by GDP – the US and China – have GINI index scores of 41.5 and 38.2 respectively. While the GINI index provides a useful starting point to consider whether development agendas are promoting equality or entrenching inequality, caution is needed as an expansion of a country's middle class may not reduce inequalities between the richest and poorest but would lead to a better GINI score.

Unlike the GINI coefficient, the Palma Ratio focuses on the inequality between the richest and poorest. To calculate a country's score, the Palma Ratio divides the income share of the top 10% by that of the bottom 40% (the middle 50% of households are seen as having a relatively stable share of national income, both over time and between countries), with the most unequal societies having higher ratios. The most unequal countries on this measure include South Africa (ratio of 6.89), Costa Rica (2.98), Chile (2.55), and Mexico (2.07), as well as the US (1.81) and UK (1.57). At the other end of the scale, the most equitable are the Slovak Republic (0.71), Slovenia (0.83), and the Czech Republic (0.84) as well as a slew of Scandinavian states (OECD, 2022).

While the Palma Ratio is useful in measuring *economic* inequalities at a *national* scale, it is unable to account for other forms of inequalities (including social, political, gender) nor can it consider inequalities at other scales (including the household). Crucially, this highlights the importance of thinking about development as more than just economic growth and economic inequalities, and of ensuring the delivery of – and equitable access to – social services as well as political, social, and economic rights and opportunities (UN, 2019). Linked to this, it is crucial to recognise and understand key sub-national patterns in inequalities, which can often be social (gender) but also spatial (rural-urban).

DEVELOPMENT AS MORE THAN ECONOMIC GROWTH

As the range of targets and indicators in both the MDGs and SDGs illustrate, there has been a mainstreaming of more holistic understandings of development. Measures of poverty have become multidimensional, with greater emphasis placed on tackling overlapping disadvantages (Alkire and Sumner, 2013) and ideas of social and environmental justice and sustainability becoming more prominent. As a result, concerns over the social and environmental sustainability of recent economic growth strategies have become more pronounced (UN, 2019).

As approaches to development have moved beyond a purely economic focus, so too have development indicators. Alongside the Multidimensional Poverty Indicator (see earlier), one of the most commonly used is the UN's Human Development Index (HDI). Developed during the 1980s and informed by Amartya Sen's work on the capabilities approach, the HDI combines multiple indicators of development covering standard of living, education and knowledge, and a long and healthy life. The final HDI score for a country – between 0 and 1, with a higher score indicative of a higher level of human development – is based on scores derived from life expectancy at birth, expected years of schooling, mean average years of schooling, and Gross National Income (GNI) per capita.

Other development indicators or measures – in addition to progress towards the SDG targets – include indices such as:

- The UN's Gender Inequality Index – which measures gender-based inequalities in reproductive health, empowerment, and the labour market.
- The Global Peace Index – which measures how 'peaceful' a country is based on ongoing conflicts, levels of insecurity, and militarisation.
- Global Corruption Index and Corruption Perceptions Index – which rank countries on (perceived) levels of corruption and associated risks.
- The UN's World Happiness Report – which ranks countries based upon quality-of-life indicators and respondents' reporting of their levels of happiness.

As outlined next, this move to looking at development – and poverty – as more than economics is tied to a broader shift towards more people-centred development approaches and theories.

SHIFTING THEORIES OF DEVELOPMENT

Ways of thinking about development have evolved over time. The early years of the development agenda were largely premised upon the role of the state and of major global institutions as the key drivers of development. These early approaches can be understood as being 'top-down' – or 'trickle-down' – in approach: in other words, development was envisioned on a grand scale, led by political or economic leaders, and focused upon major economic growth and initiatives. These, the argument went, would lead to increases in GDP and development – and while the initial accrual of wealth would occur amongst the wealthier in society, in the longer term the resultant benefits (in terms of economic growth) would 'trickle down' to ordinary citizens.

As explored in what follows, these top-down approaches to development proved of limited success, often serving to exacerbate inequalities both within and between countries. Increasing calls for 'bottom-up' development with a focus on local-level needs, priorities, input, and outcomes followed. Allied to this shift was an increased emphasis in development policy and practice on non-economic development indicators, as well as the role of communities, civil society, and social movements as drivers for development.

At the heart of 'bottom-up' development approaches were ideas of participation and empowerment. These approaches emphasised the importance of the knowledge and agency of local communities, arguing that these should be central to development policy and practice. Advocates for bottom-up and participatory development argued that dominant development agendas were guilty of imposing Western ideas, priorities, and knowledges onto local context, and sought to challenge these power dynamics and give communities the capacity to control their own lives and development (Chambers, 1986; Freire, 1993). These shifting approaches are framed by a diverse and complex history of development: to guide you through this history the following section provides a loosely chronological overview of the emergence of different schools of thought. However, it should be noted that there is tremendous overlap and interaction between approaches that cannot be captured here (for a more detailed overview, see Willis, 2021).

MODERNISATION (1950s–60s)

Amongst the most influential development theories of the post-World War II period was modernisation theory. This approach, rooted in a distinction between 'traditional' and 'modern' or 'simple' and 'complex' social and economic systems, normalised the organisational structures of Western societies, providing a heavily Eurocentric view of development (Hout, 2016).

Modernisation approaches prioritised economic growth as development, were rooted in neo-classical economics, and were framed by an optimistic view that development challenges could quickly be resolved through the sharing of expertise, finances, and technology. As a result, development projects were highly top-down in design and implementation and focused upon large-scale infrastructural, technological, and industrial projects heavily financed by international borrowing (Elliot, 2013).

Framing much of the modernist development agenda was a development model derived from Walt Rostow's (1959) paper on 'The Stages of Economic Growth'. In this paper, Rostow offered a generalised historical overview of economic growth from traditional society to an era of high consumption, via a series of five pre-set stages. Rostow's paper did not itself offer a model for development, but his analysis of the contextual factors which framed and drove economic growth in Western countries became the foundations for the 'take-off model' (which he subsequently proposed in Rostow, 1971). Proponents of the 'take-off model' argued that all countries either had already moved, or could move, from a condition of underdevelopment by meeting a series of preconditions and from a subsistence-based economy through processes of intensification and industrialisation to a mass-consumption-based economy. While Rostow's 1959 paper emphasised the importance of contextual factors and local resources in the economic development journey of each country, the application of the model overlooked this and presumed that experiences of economic growth in the West could be repeated across the globe. This meant the centrality of colonial-era extractivism in underpinning Western economic growth was overlooked, and the ideology of capitalism and economic growth were consolidated as the dominant approaches to global development.

DEPENDENCY (1960s–70s)

Emerging as a counterpoint to modernisation theory, and drawing from Marxist thinking and development experiences in Latin America, dependency theorists such as Andre Gunnar Frank, Walden Bello, and others argued that the capitalist, economic success of the global north was reliant upon the underdevelopment of the global south. Their argument was that development is globally inter-connected: for the global north to enjoy economic success, this relied upon the violence and extractivism of slavery, colonialism, and unequal trade relations with the global south. In other words, devel-opment in one region was dependent upon the underdevelopment of another, resulting in the 'development of underdevelopment' due to inherently unequal exchanges in the international capitalist system.

Dependency theorists argued that 'underdevelopment' was not a consequence of shortcomings within a country, but rather due to international trade barriers, divisions of labour, and other structural factors (Elliot, 2013). The driving force of underdevelopment is thus identified as the capitalist logic of capital accumulation through which 'the centre has been able to siphon off economic surpluses from the periphery' (Hout, 2016: 27) through forced labour and slavery, unequal trade relations, and profit flows from investments.

As a result, rather than the West offering solutions to development challenges, dependency theorists argued that not only was the West the cause of underdevelopment but it relied (and continued to rely) upon this to fuel its own development (Harriss, 2014). The continued failure of modernisation approaches to development to tackle dee-pening global inequalities ensured that the dependency approach enjoyed growing influence into the 1970s and became integral to the emergent world-system theory promoted by Immanuel Wallerstein and others. The world-system approach utilised the same underlying critique of accumulation as offered by dependency theory but placed emphasis on the role of the 'semi-periphery' as both exploiters and exploited in the capitalist world system.

STRUCTURALISM (1960s)

Influenced by dependency theory and ongoing experiences in Latin America, structuralist development approaches advocated for states to take a stronger role in directing domestic development agendas and reject the mantra of free trade. Instead, structuralists argued for a focus on domestic structural development, with governments providing strategic direction and investment to promote economic growth and import-substitution industrialisation (ISI). To realise ISI, governments needed to implement import tariffs and other measures to reduce imports to protect the development of domestic industries to supply domestic markets (contrary to free market ideology). While such policies showed success in the 1960s in providing consumer goods, they were limited by domestic market capacity and purchasing power.

BASIC NEEDS APPROACH (1970s)

The failure of modernisation policies and a focus on economic growth contributed to the emergence of other approaches to global development in the 1970s. Building on earlier arguments, the International Labour Organisation proposed a Basic Needs Approach for development and poverty reduction. Their argument was for development agendas to focus on meeting the basic needs of all as quickly as possible, with employment creation key to this. This agenda was driven, in part, by frustrations with the failures of 'trickle-down' development approaches and, instead, focused on realising the needs of the poorest – in terms of access to food, shelter, and clothing, to essential services, to paid employment, and to participation in political decision making (Willis, 2021).

However, such approaches were highly cost-intensive (for instance in delivering basic services to all) and with a focus on agricultural and urban informal economies, critics argued that these initiatives would hinder rapid economic growth and reinforced a focus on primary commodity-based economies (Willis, 2021).

WOMEN/GENDER AND DEVELOPMENT (1970s–2020s)

It was only in the 1970s that the development sector began to seriously consider the gendered impacts of development policies and practices. Benería et al. (2016) note how the mainstreaming of the Women In Development (WID) agenda (later shifting to Women And Development (WAD) and then Gender and

Development (GAD)) was driven by Ester Boserup's (1970) seminal work *Woman's Role in Economic Development*, which highlighted how women had been harmed and marginalised by modernisation, how dominant approaches undervalued the 'reproductive' (i.e. domestic and unpaid) labour completed by women, and how women were excluded from sections of the labour market.

The WID approach of the 1970s was linked to liberal feminism and critically responded to dominant thinking which positioned women as unproductive and dependent upon male wage earners. This positioning had been evident in the absence of women in development policy beyond their role as mothers and wives, which had been manifest in a 'welfare approach' to women that focused on making women 'better mothers' (Benería et al., 2016). Rejecting this position, WID provided a first step towards including and recognising women in development thinking and policy and 'promoted women's integration into the economy on an equal footing with men as the means of improving women's status in developing countries' (Benería et al., 2016: 5). As a result, a focus on women was incorporated into both bilateral and multilateral development priorities – including the UN's 1979 Convention on the Elimination of all Forms of Discrimination Against Women (CEDAW).

Moving beyond the economic focus (and paternalistic overtones) of WID, the WAD movement of the late 1970s expanded these efforts to incorporate a critical examination of the socio-economic structures that produced gendered inequalities. Informed by Marxist critiques of capital accumulation – and colonialism as a particular form of exploitative accumulation – advocates of WAD argued that the experiences of development by women (as well as children and men) were diverse and informed by class and other positionalities. As a result, WAD approaches sought to critically redress the structures which led to gendered inequalities, with greater emphasis on access, rights, and equality. More recently, the shift towards gender (and the GAD approach) rather than women has fostered critical engagements with social constructions of gender identities, interrelations, and femininities and masculinities and the importance of these within development agendas.

The importance and influence of these approaches is clear, with the continued mainstreaming of gender perspectives and targets into development policy and practice – including within the MDGs and SDGs. However, critics have noted that this mainstreaming has depoliticised the approach, stripping back concerns with justice and rights and replacing these with performative targets (Cornwall and Rivas, 2015). Further critiques have included continued tendencies to overlook intersectionality and homogenise the experience (and thus policy responses) of 'poor global south women' and struggles to move beyond a binary approach to gender (Cornwall and Rivas, 2015).

NEOLIBERALISM (1980s–2020s)

The turn to the political right in the 1980s – seen in the elected leaders of the US (Ronald Reagan), UK (Margaret Thatcher), and Germany (Helmut Kohl) – brought with it a focus on development as economic growth driven by a free-market economy. With support from the IMF, World Bank, and other multilateral agencies, this ideology called for the rolling back of the state (both in terms of state agencies and civil service as well as state-based welfare support including health and education budgets) and an emphasis on free trade to promote economic development. Backed by major bilateral donors as well as members of the Washington Consensus, neoliberal development ideology demanded an increasing market orientation of economies and a reduced role for the state. To realise this, states seeking funding from the Bretton Woods Institutions had to agree to Structural Adjustment Programmes (SAPs). These required states to undertake tax and public spending reforms (or, more simply put, these had to be reduced), commit to low government borrowing while opening up economies for trade and investment (removing protectionist tariffs, deregulating markets, etc.), and privatise public enterprises.

ANTI- AND POST-DEVELOPMENT (1980s–2010s)

By the 1980s, the failures of economic models for development led to the emergence of a series of alternative approaches. Informed by scholars including Arturo Escobar, Amartya Sen, James Ferguson, Gustavo Esteva, and others, these called for more holistic approaches to development – in which economic growth was necessary but not the sole outcome or concern. At the crux of many of these concerns was the way in which knowledge and power were/are used to construct notions of – and identify who is – developed and underdeveloped, and thus in need of being developed. Development was identified as being a form of control and power, with 'expert' knowledge from the global north imposed on countries in the global south and continually (re)producing these countries as being inferior, lacking in agency or power, and in need of development (Escobar, 1995).

In simple terms – the politics, ideology, and discourse of development were identified as *the problem* rather than the solution. To illustrate this, we can look to Arturo Escobar's (1995) work on Colombia in which he argues that until notions of poverty and development were imposed upon the country Colombia was not 'underdeveloped' – it was only with the imposing of norms from the global north that 'development' became an issue. Anti- and post-development thinkers also highlighted concerns with the inherently environmentally destructive nature of development. Consequently, various anti-development thinkers argue the entire development paradigm needs to be replaced with a fundamentally different approach to safeguard humanity's future (Drydyk, 2016).

However, critics of post- and anti-development thinking have highlighted the tendency of these approaches to homogenise and caricature development in a particular and arguably outdated way while failing to offer specific alternatives (Willis, 2021).

SUSTAINABLE DEVELOPMENT (1980s–2020s)

The roots of the sustainable development approach can be traced to environmental movements in the 1960s and early concerns over environmental destruction including the fear of the 'silent spring', acid rain, and the depletion of the ozone layer. However, the turn to sustainable development was given greater urgency and prominence by the 1987 World Commission on Environment and Development (WCED), which was tasked with developing a blueprint for achieving global sustainable development by the year 2000. The WCED's approach was founded on a belief that economic growth could continue without compromising the viability of the world's core ecosystems (Jacques, 2021). Commonly known as the Brundtland Commission report, *Our Common Future* set out the sustainable development agenda as premised on 'meet[ing] the needs of the present without compromising the ability of future generations to meet their own needs' (Brundtland, 1987: 43). At the core of this approach was a belief that development and economic growth were limited by current technologies and the capacity of ecosystems and biospheres to withstand the effect of human actions, and that future technological developments would increase the capacity for growth (Brundtland, 1987: 43; Jacques, 2021).

Arguing that poverty levels were unsustainable, the Report identified the meeting of basic needs for all and ensuring the possibility for all to fulfil their aspirations for a better life as a key development priority (Jacques, 2021). In so doing, the Report linked development and environmental policies, and stressed the need for global partnerships to realise these goals (Elliot, 2013). However, critics argue that the report was fundamentally flawed given the impossibility of reconciling the inherently contradictory goals of environmental protection and economic growth. As a result, Rist (2007) suggests the very term 'sustainable development' is an oxymoron.

Despite this critique, the report's recommendations continue to frame discussions and policies on development. They were central to the 1992 'Earth Summit' which produced the Agenda 21 document (which detailed the what, the who, and the how needed to achieve sustainable development), as well as the UN World Summit on Sustainable Development in 2002 and the Rio +20 conference in 2012 (Elliot, 2013). While multiple interpretations remain, the crux remains a focus upon how to maintain development over time.

PARTICIPATORY DEVELOPMENT APPROACHES (1990s–2020s)

Alongside the move towards more people-centred development, the 1990s and 2000s saw a dramatic rise in calls for the voices of development recipients to be foregrounded in development policy and practice. This shift towards more participatory development approaches, in which local communities are actively involved in planning and decision making, was intended to counter top-down, Eurocentric development paradigms. For proponents such as

Robert Chambers (1986) this meant 'putting the last first' and prioritising children over adults, the poor over the rich, and so on.

While such approaches aimed to disrupt dominant development paradigms and power relationships, critics cautioned that the headlong dash to adopt participatory practices resulted in a 'tyranny of participation' (Cooke and Kothari, 2001; Enns et al., 2014). This drive to have community involvement with planning and decision making seems laudable but ran into difficulties with mediating local power dynamics and the realities of everyday life. Simply put, who would (be able to) attend meetings and have their voices heard – and who was missing and why? To what extent were local communities and participants compensated for their time? Often it was the poorest and most vulnerable who either were excluded or faced insurmountable opportunity (and other) costs in participating.

CAPABILITIES APPROACH (1990s–2010s)

Emerging in the late 1990s and part of the people-centred development turn, the capabilities approach gained significant following and influence. Driven by the work of economist Amartya Sen, the capabilities approach focuses on development as freedoms, and identifies poverty as being a lack of capabilities which limits one's ability to function in society and thus to achieve life goals. In other words, Sen (1999) does not define poverty in material terms, but as being the deprivation of basic capabilities (or freedoms).

With strong parallels to the UN's (1995) definition of overall poverty, the capabilities approach is thus concerned with removing 'unfreedoms' – whether these be poverty, tyranny, denial of political and civil rights, discrimination, or lack of access to quality education or health-care (Sen, 1999). Key freedoms – such as being able to receive basic education and health-care or to vote – are seen as the '*constituent components* of development' rather than outcomes of development processes (Sen, 1999: 5, italics in original). In other words, the capabilities approach focuses on what someone is able to be and do (what they have the possibility and ability to achieve). Rather than being concerned with what (material wealth) someone has, emphasis is placed on the freedom of the individual to use a resource and achieve an outcome

(Saigaran et al., 2015). Taking this further, Martha Nussbaum identified ten central human capabilities (including life, bodily health, bodily integrity, senses and imagination, emotions, control over one's environment, and so on) to further consider how external conditions can interact with one's internal capabilities to frame the experience of freedoms.

Crucially, this approach recognises and emphasises that individuals are not passive recipients of development but instead are agents of development – however, their agency (or freedoms) may be constrained by structural or other factors. In turn, this has allowed for deeper engagement with intersectional factors (such as age, gender, caste, geographical location, and so on) which may enable or hinder the realisation of or access to freedoms.

RIGHTS-BASED DEVELOPMENT (1990s–2010s)

The rights-based approach positions humans as the 'ends' of development. In other words, rather than locating humans as the means to realise an end (economic growth) this approach sees the provision and realisation of human rights (freedom of speech, of participation, from violence, and so on) as the ultimate goal of development. Advocates argue for the importance of every human person being able to live with dignity and emphasise the crucial role of the state in delivering and implementing legal and social protections required to ensure this is possible.

This approach has become increasingly prominent in global development in the rhetoric of many donors, and in the imposing of aid conditionalities aimed at protecting and promoting human rights. More broadly, the emphasis on rights as part of global development is rooted in the UN Declaration of Human Rights which sets out a universal set of rights which are increasingly embedded in national and global legal systems. The rights set out in the Declaration encompass social, political, economic, and civil rights, and are identified as being inalienable to all people, legally protected, and intended to ensure the equality and dignity of all. Crucially, it is incumbent (in principle at least) upon states not only to respect these rights, but also to take measures to protect them and adopt measures to ensure they are fulfilled. However, critics would argue that these commitments to human rights are rarely enforced or enacted, as geopolitical and geostrategic priorities trump human rights in development practice. The retreat from the liberal internationalism of the 1990s – when human rights were at the heart of many development agendas – underscores these concerns.

Nonetheless, rights-based approaches to development remain influential and focus upon efforts to realise systems of rights and obligations between citizens and states to promote sustainable outcomes, community empowerment, and the realisation of individual (and collective) freedoms and well-being. With strong resonance to Sen's work on capabilities, rights-based approaches seek to shift the focus and rhetoric of development away from 'needs' and on to the equal realisation of rights of access and power.

POST-COLONIAL (2000s–2020s)

The growth of post-colonial theory in the late twentieth century brought a renewed critical focus to development studies, problematising and critiquing the dominance of discourses and approaches to development from the global north. Integral to these engagements are influences of poststructuralism and Marxism which have driven a focus on how 'dominant groups in society come to exercise power and authority over less powerful or subjugated groups' – with an emphasis on both race and class, and the ways in which power is manifest in culture, politics, and economics at multiple scales (McEwan, 2009: 27).

Crucially, post-colonial engagements with development have queried the meaning of 'development' – shifting the focus from poverty to inequality (Noxolo, 2016) – while emphasising the interconnections between global north and global south, and how these interconnections constitute and perpetuate inequalities as well as representations and definitions of 'here' and 'there', 'developed' and 'underdeveloped', and so on. Post-colonial approaches to development have also generated critiques of the Eurocentrism of development studies and practice, and the role of power (in various forms) in entrenching idea(l)s and geographies of development (McEwan, 2009). Linked to these critiques, post-colonial approaches to development have (re)emphasised both the importance of 'voices, knowledges and agency in the South' *and* the reality that development concerns are relevant in every country, not just the global south (McEwan, 2009: 30). Fundamentally, as Noxolo (2016: 43) summarises, post-colonial approaches to development are concerned with contesting 'the terms and conditions of global wealth and wealth-making – its roots and complicity in colonial oppression, and its continued reproduction through exploitation, inequality and the silencing of cultural difference' to deliver sustainable global equality.

BUEN VIVIR (2000S–2020S)

A set of approaches originating in Latin America and emerging in response to failures of classical development interventions, Buen Vivir approaches development as concerned with 'the good life' or 'good living'. Drawing upon indigenous traditions and knowledge, Buen Vivir offers a counterpoint to Western developmentalism, focusing upon the realisation of improved quality of life as part of a community and as a part of nature. With strong parallels to post-development thinking, Buen Vivir is rooted in the recognition and rejection of both the social and environmental costs of classical development and the cultural knowledges which underpin these. By working with multiple cultural knowledges, Buen Vivir has evolved in a number of ways: embedded as Vivir Bien in the Bolivian constitution as a set of ethical principles including unity, dignity, reciprocity, and social justice; or expressed as a set of rights including health, environment, shelter, and education in the Buen Vivir regime in Ecuador (Gudynas, 2011). These approaches reject growth as the dominant mode for development, instead focusing upon the realisation of a sustainable, collective quality of life which serves local needs (including environmental needs) ahead of those of global markets, material production, and consumption (Campodónico et al., 2017).

CLOSING COMMENTS

As this chapter has illustrated, global development is an evolving and contested arena – one which is infused with politics, power, and ideology: determining who has the power to decide what development 'is' and how it is measured, which political agendas dominate the development landscape and agendas of major donors, and so on. While only providing a very partial and abbreviated overview of some of the changes in theoretical approaches to and ways of measuring development, this chapter illustrates the continued influence of key ideals and ideologies which remain at the forefront of debates over the focus, function, and ethics of global development.

REFERENCES

Alkire, S., Sumner, A. (2013). Multidimensional poverty and the post-2015 MDGs. *Development*, 56 (1): 46–51.

Benería, L., Berik, G., Floro, M. (2016). *Gender, Development and Globalization: Economics as if All People Mattered*. Abingdon: Routledge.

Boserup, E. (1970). *Woman's Role in Economic Development*. London: George Allen and Unwin.

Brundtland, G.H. (1987). Our common future—call for action. *Environmental Conservation*, 14 (4): 291–294.

Campodónico, H., Carbonnier, G., Vázquez, S. (2017). Alternative development narratives, policies and outcomes in the Andean Region. In Carbonnier, G., Campodónico, H., Vázquez, S. (eds) *Alternative Pathways to Sustainable Development: Lessons from Latin America* (pp. 3–15). Leiden: Brill.

Chambers, R. (1986). *Whose Reality Counts? Putting the First Last*. London: Intermediate Technology Publications.

Chancel, L., Pikkety, T., Saez, E., Zucman, G. (2022). *World Inequality Report 2022*. Paris: World Inequality Lab, UNDP.

Collier, P. (2008). *The Bottom Billion: Why the Poorest Countries are Failing and What Can Be Done about it*. Oxford: Oxford University Press.

Cooke, B., Kothari, U. (eds) (2001). *Participation: The New Tyranny?* London: Zed Books.

Cornwall, A., Rivas, A.-M. (2015). From 'gender equality and 'women's empowerment' to global justice: Reclaiming a transformative agenda for gender and development. *Third World Quarterly*, 36 (2): 396–415.

Drydyk, J. (2016). Ethical issues in development. In Grugel, J., Hammett, D. (eds) *The Palgrave Handbook of International Development* (pp. 55–76). London: Palgrave Macmillan.

Elliot, J. (2013). *An Introduction to Sustainable Development*. Abingdon: Routledge.

Enns, C., Bersaglio, B., Keep, T. (2014). Indigenous voices and the making of the post-2015 development agenda: The recurring tyranny of participation. *Third World Quarterly*, 35 (3): 358–375.

Escobar, P. (1995). *Encountering Development: The Making and Unmaking of the Third World*. Princeton, NJ: Princeton University Press.

Freire, P. (1993). *Pedagogy of the Oppressed*. London: Penguin.

Fukuda-Parr, S. (2019). Keeping out extreme inequality from the SDGs agenda – the politics of indicators. *Global Policy*, 10 (1): 61–69.

Golding, I., Reinert, K. (2012). *Globalization for Development: Meeting New Challenges*. Oxford: Oxford University Press.

Gordon, D., Levitas, R., Pantazis, C., Patsios, D., Payne, S., Townsend, P., Adelman, L., Ashworth, K., Middleton, S., Bradshaw, J., Williams, J. (2000). *Poverty and Social Exclusion in Britain*. York: Joseph Rowntree Foundation. https:// www.jrf.org.uk/sites/default/files/jrf/migrated/files/185935128x.pdf (retrieved 21/03/2023).

Gudynas, E. (2011). Buen Vivir: Today's tomorrow. *Development*, 54 (4): 441– 447.

Harriss, J. (2014). Development theories. In Currie-Alder, B., Kanbur, R., Malone, D.M., Medhora, R. (eds) *International Development: Ideas, Experience, and Prospects* (pp. 35–49). Oxford: Oxford University Press.

Hout, W. (2016). Classical approaches to development: Modernisation and dependency. In Grugel, J., Hammett, D. (eds) *The Palgrave Handbook of International Development* (pp. 21–40). London: Palgrave Macmillan.

Hulme, D. (2003). Chronic poverty and development policy: An introduction. *World Development*, 31 (3): 399–402.

Hussain, M.A. (2020). Absolute poverty. In Greve, B. (ed) *Routledge International Handbook of Poverty* (pp. 11–23). Abingdon: Routledge.

Jacques, P. (2021). *Sustainability: The Basics*. Abingdon: Routledge.

Jefferson, P. (2020). Global poverty: Trends, measures and antidotes. In Greve, B. (ed) *Routledge International Handbook of Poverty* (pp. 119–129). Abingdon: Routledge.

McEwan, C. (2009). *Postcolonialism and Development*. Abingdon: Routledge.

Noxolo, P. (2016). Postcolonial approaches to development. In Grugel, J., Hammett, D. (eds) *The Palgrave Handbook of International Development* (pp. 41–53). London: Palgrave Macmillan.

OECD (2022). Income inequality (indicator). Paris: OECD. doi:10.1787/ 459aa7f1-en (retrieved 08/07/2022).

OPHI (2021). Global MPI 2021. Oxford: Oxford Poverty & Human Development Initiative, Oxford Department of International Development. https:// ophi.org.uk/global-mpi-2021/ (retrieved 14/03/2023).

Rist, G. (2007). Development as a buzzword. *Development in Practice*, 17 (4/5): 485–491.

Rostow, W. (1959). The stages of economic growth. *The Economic History Review*, 12 (1): 1–16.

Rostow, W. (1971). The take-off into self-sustained growth. In Mountjoy, A. B. (ed) *Developing the Underdeveloped Countries* (pp. 86–114). London: Palgrave Macmillan.

Sachs, J. (2005). *The End of Poverty: How We Can Make it Happen in Our Lifetime*. London: Penguin UK.

Saigaran, N.G., Karupiah, P., Gopal, P.S. (2015). The capability approach: Comparing Amartya Sen and Martha Nussbaum. In *Touching Lives, Bridging Society. Proceedings of University Sains Malaysia International Conference on Social Sciences* (pp. 1–8). Pulau Pinang, Malaysia: Universiti Sains Malaysia.

Sen, A. (1999). *Development as Freedom*. Oxford: Oxford University Press.

UN (1995). *Final Report of the World Summit for Social Development*. New York: United Nations.

UN (2019). *The Future is Now: Science for Achieving Sustainable Development – Global Sustainable Development Report 2019*. New York: United Nations.

UN Women (2022). Poverty deepens for women and girls, according to latest projections. New York: UN Women. https://data.unwomen.org/features/p overty-deepens-women-and-girls-according-latest-projections (retrieved 14/ 03/2023).

Willis, K. (2021). *Theories and Practices of Development*. Abingdon: Routledge.

4

GLOBALISATION, ECONOMICS, AND DEVELOPMENT

Global development is inherently entwined with various relations, networks, and connections spanning the globe and involving both state and non-state actors. From the historic evolution of trade relations and economics through the defining and imposing of development agendas to agreements about climate change and sustainability, networks of actors are involved. These actors – and flows of various forms of capital between them – are increasingly interconnected at a global scale. Whether in flows of news or cultural influences, circulations of money through global markets, or in the journey(s) of the items that make up your breakfast or your wardrobe, flows of goods, services, finance, ideas, and people around the world are integral to the history, present, and future of global development.

GLOBALISATION

This intensification of connections between states is commonly referred to as *globalisation*: the processes through which markets expand across national borders as communication, travel, and interconnections between states increase in intensity and speed due to advances in transport and communication technologies. In popular language, these processes are also known as 'time-space compression' or the 'shrinking' of the world as flows of information, goods, and people have sped up, 'reducing' the (temporal) distance between parts of the globe.

The resulting increased exchanges in economic, social, and cultural capital have contributed to greater economic interdependence

DOI: 10.4324/9781003155652-4

and fundamental shifts in the global economy and societal relations. Subsequent flows and exchanges between peoples and places include the economic, social, cultural, political, technological and virtual, environmental, human (personal mobility), as well as biological. Crucially, these different types of flows are often interconnected. Think for instance of the spread of diseases with the movement of people, plants, and animals around the world: from smallpox to Covid.

As the mention of smallpox suggests, globalisation has a much longer history than its current phase from the 1980s to the present, a phase which is indelibly liked with neoliberal capitalism. Empire and imperialism were inherently entwined with globalisation, as improvements to travel (railways, steamships, etc.) and communications facilitated global trade and colonial conquest. This period was marked by international flows of people, of colonial officials moving from the colonial powers to the colonies and the forced movement of enslaved Africans away from their homelands, as well as of goods and materials – natural resources from the colonies to the colonial powers, manufactured goods from colonial powers to the colonies. These flows facilitated colonial expansion and the economic growth of colonial powers, generating huge wealth not only for port cities in the UK such as Bristol and Liverpool (which were key hubs of the slave trade) but also for those producing the chains, weapons, and other materials used to maintain the slave trade and colonial rule (McEwan, 2009).

The legacies of this phase of globalisation, during which colonialism dominated and directed connections and flows between colonial powers and colonies in particular and extractive ways, remain influential to this day. Viewing colonies as sources of raw materials (primary commodities) to be extracted and exploited, colonial authorities shaped the infrastructure and development of their colonies to promote extractive industries and trade routes. Roads, railways, and other infrastructure were developed to move goods (and people) from the 'interior' of a colony to key trading ports, from where these goods were shipped to the colonial power. As a result, internal transport networks and links to neighbouring states were often neglected, a challenge which post-colonial governments have been tasked with addressing.

These extractive practices also embedded particular trading relations, such that the colonies were spaces for the extraction of primary commodities to be shipped to the colonial power for use in manufacturing, before manufactured goods were sold back to the colonies. This historical process remains – in broad terms – in place today as many countries in the global south continue to rely upon exports of raw materials (from oil to cocoa, timber to groundnuts). As explored in further detail later, this continued reliance places these national economies at risk of market turbulence and sudden drops in demand and commodity prices (such as cocoa) as well as making them vulnerable to crop or other failures.

More broadly, advances in air travel, modern shipping, and communication technologies have contributed to shifting patterns of migration, economic investment, trade flows, labour outsourcing, cultural exchanges, and other forms of interconnection. The shifting landscape of globalisation means that the outcomes and experiences of globalisation are both highly varied (differing levels of connectivity to global networks and flows) and strongly connected (in the experience of the imposition of development agendas and economic orthodoxy through the global reach of international organisations and financial institutions).

To help us understand the complexity of these variations and interconnections, Potter et al. (2012) provide a useful outline of 12 (interconnected) dimensions of contemporary globalisation (Box 4.1). Their approach highlights not only the multiple layers and forms of interconnections and actors involved in these networks and flows, but also how these facilitate and support the spread and influence of dominant political and economic ideology and power across the globe. As a result, we can also recognise why globalisation is such a divisive concept and process.

BOX 4.1 TWELVE DIMENSIONS OF GLOBALISATION

i *Financial globalisation* – facilitated by the 24/7 global finance market and deregulation of the sector which has increased the speed, ease, and quantity of financial flows between national jurisdictions and economies.

ii *Globalisation of corporate power* – the rise and expansion of MNCs and TNCs, many of which have more political power and wealth than some nation states.

iii *Technological globalisation* – the rapid expansion of ICTs has contributed to 'time-space compression' as well as a growing digital divide between those with and those without ICT access.

iv *Political globalisation* – the spread of neoliberal orthodoxy and expectation that governments will support free-market ideology.

v *Economic globalisation* – the growth of transnational production networks and logistical and communication systems supporting these.

vi *Ecological globalisation* – the expansion of ecologically focused civil society organisations and efforts to protect the environment at a global or transnational scale.

vii *Globalisation of labour* – both the circulation and contrasting mobilities of high- and low-skilled workforces moving across national borders, and the offshoring of labour by companies through the New International Division of Labour (NIDL).

viii *Illegal globalisation* – the rise in illegal trade and smuggling networks and organised crime, from poaching of endangered species to human trafficking to drugs cartels and arms smugglers.

ix *Cultural globalisation* – the spread and influence of popular culture, not only the Coca-Cola-isation associated with American cultural hegemony but the counter-flows of influences from the Caribbean, Latin America, Asia, and Africa into Western popular culture.

x *Globalisation of fear and conflict* – associated with the 'war on terror' and the emphasis on homeland security to justify overseas military interventions.

xi *Globalisation from below* – the spread and networking of anti-globalisation movements around the world.

xii *Geographical globalisation* – the increasing influence on international institutions and cross-border practices which, for the wealthy and for capital, have led to an increasingly borderless world (which, simultaneously, has led to an increasingly bordered world for the poor and marginal).

Source: Potter et al. (2012: 87–89)

On the one hand, advocates for globalisation argue that these processes drive economic growth and opportunities, facilitate social and cultural exchange, and support development. On the other, critics such as Benería et al. (2016) argue that the processes of economic integration have led to increased individualism, marketisation, and commercialisation – with profound implications for individual and social well-being and global sustainability, and the entrenching of inequalities and injustices. Their argument is that rather than supporting growth and development, globalisation sustained continued dominance by the global north, the accrual of wealth by elites, and adherence to a neoliberal economic orthodoxy. Providing a powerful insight into these interconnections between globalisation and neoliberal economic orthodoxy, Cindi Katz (2004) outlines how young people in seemingly disparate countries (the US and Sudan) face similar life challenges arising from neoliberal economic development agendas, shifting employment markets, and changing social practices. More widely, the twin drivers of globalisation and neoliberal capitalism are viewed as contributing to continued inequalities and unequal revenue flows which maintain existing global core–periphery dynamics through inequitable flows of trade, knowledge, finance, and skills.

FROM KEYNESIAN CAPITALISM TO NEOLIBERALISM

A key term that is frequently used in discussions of globalisation, economics, and development is 'neoliberalism'. It is so widely used that its meaning is often taken for granted and ends up being used as a catch-all phrase for capitalist economic systems and thinking. Such an approach is lazy: to critically engage with economics and development it is important to understand what neoliberalism is, how it differs from previous incarnations of capitalism, how this ideology has permeated so much of the global development sector, and why it has emerged as such a divisive and (often) detested concept for many social justice and global development activists.

Before exploring neoliberalism, we first need to understand what it replaced – namely a previous approach to capitalism, Keynesian economics. Named after its main proponent, John Maynard Keynes, Keynesian economics was itself a response to the Great Depression of the 1930s. At its core, Keynesianism argued that the key driver of economic growth was overall demand (how much households, government, and business spent) and that governments played a key role in maintaining and promoting national economies. Crucially, Keynesian economists argued that the free market lacked a self-balancing mechanism, meaning the state played a vital role in promoting (full) employment and economic stability, including the provision of welfare and public services in sectors that the private sector didn't see as suitably profitable. In policy terms, this was commonly seen in the provision of heavily subsidised or free-at-point-of-use services in health, education, and public infrastructure.

This approach, however, fell out of favour following the global economic crisis of the late 1970s and early 1980s. This crisis was triggered by the 1970s OPEC (Organisation of Petroleum Exporting Countries) crisis and the decision by countries – initially the US in 1971 – to move away from fixed exchange rates and the gold standard (when the value of a currency was based on a particular quantity of gold). The abandoning of the gold standard meant currencies became a speculative, tradable commodity for the first time. These changes, alongside the OPEC crisis, combined to trigger the 1979–1983 recession and the end of the dominance of Keynesian economics.

In the wake of this turmoil, the supply-side, free-market capitalist ideology known as neoliberalism was eagerly embraced by conservative politicians of the day – in particular, US President Ronald Reagan and UK Prime Minister Margaret Thatcher – as well as the World Bank and IMF. Promoted by University of Chicago economists Fredrick von Hayek and Milton Friedman, neoliberalism prioritises individual freedom as the ultimate political good and one that can only be realised through a competitive market economy which is free from state interference – the state's role reduced to serving the market by ensuring that the conditions for a free market exist (Harrison, 2010).

Quickly becoming the dominant economic ideology in the Western world, this approach resulted in drastic cuts to government budgets; the privatising of social services, infrastructure, and state entities (such as telecoms companies, railways, water supplies, etc.); the removal of trade barriers and tariffs (called trade liberalisation); and reductions in controls on capital flows (i.e. Foreign

Direct Investment (FDI)) (Benería et al., 2016). The effects of this policy agenda have been seen across the globe – from trade relations (covered in more detail later) to the 'austerity' politics in the US and Europe following the 2008 economic recession and the quest to eliminate budget deficits by cutting public spending rather than raising taxes.

Within the global development sector, the World Bank's (1981) Berg Report (officially titled *Accelerated Development in Sub-Saharan Africa: An Agenda to Action*) linked the development 'failures' of African states to previous failures to adopt free-market economics. The solution to these 'failures'? A neoliberal free-market agenda – and this was then reflected in the World Bank and IMF's Structural Adjustment Programme (SAP) approach to supporting global development.

While neoliberal economic logic has influenced policies around the world, the effects of these policies have been inequitably realised. Crucially, neoliberalism has fetishised growth and accumulation – the mantra that more is better, that growth is both the means and outcome of development. This has led to an intensification and acceleration of production and consumption with little interest in or commitment to the sustainability of these processes. The result? An obsession with rapid growth and short-termism that is inherently unsustainable and fundamentally incompatible with either a sustainable development agenda or a sustainable future for humanity on the planet.

Compounding these concerns are the inequitable and unjust outcomes of neoliberal policies which primarily benefit economic elites and international finance, rather than the wishes and needs of everyday citizens. These concerns are particularly prominent in relation to FDI related to extractive industries (mining, oil, etc.). Accounting for large proportions of overall FDI flows into many countries, rather than supporting sustainable, long-term national economic growth, these investments often result in the offshoring of profits to investors (and their shareholders) and the enrichment of a small local elite, while communities face dispossession of land and the costs of social and environmental damage.

Further exacerbating these concerns is the view that neoliberal agendas have been inequitably imposed upon post-colonial and post-Communist states which have been required to open up markets and economies to Western investors to a much greater extent than Western countries have been compelled to do. This resulted in the entrenching of existing global core–periphery divides and imposition of neoliberal agendas through donor funding requirements that stipulated the need for recipient countries to undertake policy changes to promote free-market economics, or risk facing punitive measures including reducing or cutting aid payments or credit lines and ratings (Benería et al., 2016; Harrison, 2010).

More broadly, the pressures to reduce 'barriers' to business and roll back the state are often manifest through the removal of environmental and workers' protections and regressive tax regimes. Consequently, everyday citizens are often faced with deepening inequalities, greater precarity, the impacts of environmental and ecological destruction, land grabs and enclosures, and the privatisation and exploitation of public and natural resources, utilities, and housing. Again, these concerns are not restricted to the global south – witness the failures of the privatisation of water suppliers in the UK where privatised corporations extract vast profits for (often overseas) investors while failing to adequately maintain and upgrade aging supply systems and releasing untreated sewage into rivers and the sea.

Elsewhere, the role of the private sector in providing water supplies has also been controversial. In the face of rapid (and informal) urbanisation across many countries in the global south, the provision of basic services – specifically water – became a priority for the World Bank, donors, and national governments. Throughout the 1970s and 1980s, support focused upon (local) government development of infrastructure and supplies of 'public' water. However, the landscape of water provision remained complex – with households accessing a mixture of 'public' water as well as 'private' suppliers (whether through household wells, local water vendors, tanker-trucks, etc.). In reality, as Bakker (2013) outlines, the provision of public water supplies to everyone in cities in the global south was – and still is – a pipe-dream. As a result, governments focused on providing public water supplies to wealthy residents while relying upon 'private' providers (including profit-makers) to take responsibility for water delivery in poor communities. Thus, recognising 'who has clean safe water, and who does not, reveals the workings of power around the world' (Sultana, 2020: 1407). Issues with unaffordable price increases, failures in delivery, and a lack of accountability of private providers have since led to various conflicts and protests, including the famous Cochabamba 'water war' in Bolivia between 1999 and 2000.

Despite such problems, supporters argue that neoliberalism has promoted, and will continue to promote, global economic development. But is there evidence to support these claims? Evidence of the success of neoliberal development policies in promoting economic growth and development is limited – not least on the continent of Africa. Since the first structural adjustments were imposed on Senegal in 1979 to promote economic liberalisation, dozens of other African countries have reached adjustment agreements with the World Bank and IMF in return for development finance (Harrison, 2010). These agreements commonly included requirements for recipient states to open their economies to FDI, remove price controls, reduce public (social) spending, and remove currency exchange controls (which often led to the devaluation of currencies, thereby making things more expensive to import and increasing costs of living) (Harrison, 2010: 39). These policies left many economies stagnant or in decline; contributed to huge increases in external debt burdens; dramatic reductions in spending on health, education, and welfare; and rendered working lives and livelihoods increasingly insecure and precarious, leaving average citizens poorer and increasing numbers living in poverty: between 1981 and 2001, the number of those living in poverty doubled to 313 million (Harrison, 2010: 39).

Over time, the major donors have acknowledged that the neoliberal agenda as implemented via SAPs was not working. However, rather than seeking a new economic orthodoxy or approach, a new form of structural adjustments was introduced under the guise of the HIPC (Heavily Indebted Poor Countries) initiative of the 1990s. The HIPC initiative required recipients to commit to structural adjustments in order to reduce external debt levels and qualify for debt relief to then release funds for social expenditure on health and education. Parallel to the HIPCs, PRSPs (Poverty Reduction Strategy Papers) emerged as a replacement for SAPs and included more of a focus on social spending.

ALTERNATIVES TO NEOLIBERALISM: THE DEVELOPMENTAL STATE

Contrasting with the dominant market-based development models of the West, the East Asian model of development is premised upon a belief that the market is not always effective in promoting economic development. Instead, the government is seen as needing to provide vital interventions to stimulate particular aspects of economic growth and development. As a result, this approach is also referred to as the Developmental State Model (Leftwich, 1995; Wylde, 2016), and has been seen in Japan, South Korea, Vietnam, Singapore, and China.

This model of development sees a government strategically investing in aspects of the economy (through both state-owned enterprises and private corporations) to promote economic growth and export revenues, which in turn also attract foreign direct investment. Tax breaks, financial support for banks and companies, tight control over trade unions and broader civil and political rights, as well as investments in infrastructure (from education to roads to energy) are all used to support economic growth – often linked to technological developments and a move to a consumer-based economy. In other words, the state is seen as key to harnessing national and international forces to realise development outcomes – with targeted industrialisation a key part of this strategy.

While the developmental state model has been successful in many ways, it also contributed to the East Asian financial crisis of the late 1990s. Due to the success of this approach in driving the rapid economic growth of Singapore (Box 4.2), Taiwan, and South Korea, the developmental state approach has been adopted (to varying degrees, and with rather more limited success) by Paul Kagame in Rwanda and Yoweri Museveni in Uganda, as well as in Argentina, Brazil, and Ethiopia. This approach has historical precedence in (pre-)colonial periods, when the state and state technocrats were positioned as the only ones who knew how to realise development outcomes. However, these historical efforts were often allied with racism and other forms of discrimination, as colonial narratives argued that state institutions needed to overcome or destroy other social structures and relations in order to realise development.

BOX 4.2   SINGAPORE – THE DEVELOPMENTAL STATE

One of the icons of the developmental state approach is Singapore, the 'little red dot'. Following independence from Britain in 1965, the Singaporean government feared invasion and colonisation by Malaysia. As a result, Singaporean political leaders focused upon securing the nation's independence and promoting sustained economic growth. As a result of total political control over the island nation being held by the People's Action Party, the government was able to make strategic investments to move the country's economy from cottage industry through small-scale industry and into being an industrial economy. Core to these efforts were government strategies to use tax and other inducements to gain investment from overseas alongside the use of political, legal, and ideological tools to promote ideals of citizenship which marginalised dissent and activism, and instilled a sense of cooperation for realisation of benefits. This process was aided by the availability of a well-educated but low-paid workforce.

The result? A sustained period of 15% economic growth per annum between 1965 and 1980. And then, in the period since, a coordinated move to a service-based, biotechnology, and hydro-technology economy. In short, this success relied (and continues to rely) upon a determined and autonomous (political) elite, a weak civil society, and effective management of other interests and suppressions of dissent and opposition. Economic power is used to promote development by subsidies and investments, while political power is used to demobilise civil society and ensure popular support and compliance.

ALTERNATIVES TO NEOLIBERALISM: DEGROWTH, GREEN GROWTH, AND THE CIRCULAR ECONOMY

Critics of the failures of neoliberalism to realise sustainable, equitable growth and development have identified a range of development economics alternatives. Prominent amongst these are ideas of degrowth, green growth, and the circular economy.

Proponents for a degrowth approach argue that the current neoliberal, consumption-driven approach to development and growth is fundamentally unsustainable. These concerns are reflected in the movement of 'overshoot day' (the day on which we use all the biological resources that the planet produces in a year): in 2022 it was 28 July, compared to early August in 2012, mid-October in 1992, and mid-November in 1982. In broad terms, in 1971 the world's population consumed approximately 1 Earth's worth of biological resources – by 2022 this figure was 1.75 Earths' worth of resources. (You can work out your own ecological footprint and overshoot day here: https://www.footprintcalculator.org/home/en.)

Advocates for degrowth therefore call for an economic model which involves a 'planned reduction of energy and resource use designed to bring the economy back into balance with the living world in a way that reduces inequality and improves human well-being' (Hickel, 2021: 1105). While the name 'degrowth' is often understood in economic terms, the core focus is not on shrinking economies but rather on reducing throughput and consumption of (natural) resources and energy while moving away from the obsession with economic growth.

At the heart of these concerns are a set of basic questions: Do rich countries need more growth? Do you need another (fast fashion) outfit for a night out? Do you need the latest smartphone if your current one is working OK?

To be realised effectively, degrowth would need to be carefully planned, with a potential initial focus on reducing the most ecologically damaging (and socially least important) production processes (e.g. luxury cars, arms, planned obsolescence, beef farming) while investing in care, education, and community. Alongside this, advocates argue that governments would need to emphasise efforts to improve employment (e.g. reducing working hours/weeks, retraining for new sectors) as well as efforts to restore and promote biodiversity and improve 'well-being' rather than 'material wealth'. While critics have argued that such efforts may place an unfair burden upon countries in the global south, advocates have taken care to argue that, as 92% of carbon dioxide emissions above the planetary threshold are emitted by those in the global north, efforts to realise degrowth should be focused on those in the global north alongside a commitment to social justice and supporting sustainable development in the global south (Hickel, 2021).

Meanwhile, green growth advocates argue for an approach to economic growth that is based on the protection and restoration of the environment. Originally surfacing in the 1990s, the more recent political emphasis on promoting low-carbon, socially inclusive development has seen green growth ideas becoming more mainstream. Central to this approach is a focus on environmental investments – in renewable energy, rewilding projects, and the prevention of climate change. In political circles these ideas have been incorporated into talk of 'green jobs' or a 'green new deal', with policies and economic support to be aimed at replacing sunset (harmful) with sunrise (net positive) industries, supporting green technologies, and a move towards consuming less.

The idea of the 'circular economy' is also based in ecological principles and a reduction in extraction from nature. As the name suggests, the circular economy approach calls for a shift away from linear economy in which raw materials are extracted from the environment, used, and then disposed of or thrown away, to one in which waste becomes the resource to then be used – and so on. While there is growing support for this approach in some political and industrial circles, critics have cautioned that not all industries can be made 'circular' and that this move may result in unintended externalities that fuel climate change and social exclusion. However, it remains one of the more readily understandable approaches and has clear potential to support the realisation of various SDG targets and measures (for instance, SDG 12.5: 'By 2030, substantially reduce waste generation through prevention, reduction, recycling and reuse').

ALTERNATIVES TO NEOLIBERALISM: NATURAL RESOURCE RENTS (OR THE 'RESOURCE CURSE')

Other options pursued by countries to support development agendas include exploitation of natural resources (often called 'natural resource rents') to raise revenues from oil, gas, export agriculture, mineral mining, etc. This may be done by state-owned or parastatal companies, or by private (often overseas) companies operating under concessions or licenses with the state then generating revenue from concession fees and tax revenues. Advocates note this approach reduces the dependency of states on International Financial Institutions (IFIs) and other donors (and their conditionalities), allowing a reorientation away from aid and towards trade as a means of economic growth and supporting development. The role of the BRICS is often seen as key here (Carmody, 2008) – and while pre-Covid commodity booms were reducing the aid dependency of some countries, they remain(ed) exposed to the risk of market volatilities.

In some countries, efforts have been made to ring-fence natural resource rents (particularly from mining) to social investment and welfare spending. However, sustainability questions remain, not only in terms of how long will resources last, but in terms of pollution and environmental damage, as well as concerns over working conditions and treatment of workers and human rights violations. Thus, many consider natural resources as being a double-edged sword for development: they may generate revenues but these do not necessarily promote development and growth. Indeed, some talk of the 'resource curse' (Haarstad, 2016), arguing that an abundance of mineral or other natural resources results in lower overall economic growth (as the dominance of the sector closes the space for other economic development), increases risks of violence and conflict, and that the 'plunder economy' of colonialism may be reinforced (Carmody, 2008). These risks, Belaid et al. (2021) argue, are much greater in states with a military ruler than those without. More broadly, Carmody (2008) cautions that natural resource rents can undermine the potential for a social contract between citizens and the state (the state can raise revenues from extractive practices without the need to develop a 'tax contract' with citizens), while also driving social and spatial inequalities as the economic benefits accrue to a small elite while the environmental, social, and other costs of extractive industries are felt by local communities.

FINANCIAL FLOWS

Integral to the pursuit of neoliberal global development policies are flows of finance. These flows include ODA, remittances, as well as four major types of global financial flow: *foreign direct investment*

(investment into a foreign-based business or enterprise through which the investor takes at least 10% ownership of the business), *equity investment* (investment in (i.e. purchasing of) shares in a foreign business), *bond finance* (bonds are issued by governments or corporations to raise money from investors in the form of a loan which the bond issuer then repays. Investors face the risk of loans not being repaid (known as 'defaulting'), meaning companies and countries seek to develop and improve their *credit rating* in order to attract investors), and *bank lending* (governments or corporations borrow money from commercial banks) (Goldin, 2018). Totalling hundreds of billions of dollars each year, these flows provide significant financial support for global development. However, critics caution that these flows can also undermine or restrict development – for instance, if a country's debt load rises it can become an unsustainable drain on government spending and money that could have been used on education, health, infrastructure, or other projects ends up being spent 'servicing' government debts (explored in more detail later). When this becomes acute, a state may default on either bond finance or bank lending, making it harder (and more expensive) to secure further development finance. Crucially, states need to balance short- and longer-term interests: FDI and equity finance inflows may stimulate growth and development in the immediate term, but the danger is that longer-term finance flows are outwards via the offshoring of profits to overseas 'parent' companies and investors.

THE NEW INTERNATIONAL DIVISION OF LABOUR

Alongside major flows in finance, we have also witnessed a different type of flow – the flow of particular types of work (rather than workers, who are discussed in the section on migration) around the globe as a result of the increased interconnectivity of globalisation. Known as the New International Division of Labour (NIDL), this process emerged in response to the 1970s economic crisis as companies sought to reduce costs and survive the global recession by moving large parts of their manufacturing and other activities to the global south. This global shift in the geography of work, across multiple economic sectors – evident in the shift in manufacturing to China or the locating of major companies' call-centres in (for instance) India – has been driven by companies seeking the benefits of lower wages and decreased legal protection of workers' rights and environmental controls.

More recently, the NIDL is evident in the global spread of the 'gig economy' and 'platform working', where digital work (such as coding, programming, and other IT-based work) is outsourced to workers across the globe – often working in precarious conditions, subject to algorithmic monitoring, and with low wages. These online labour markets or platforms connect demands for digital skills in Western Europe and North America with labour supplies elsewhere in the world – often in Eastern Europe and South Asia – at a far lower cost than employing workers in Western Europe or North America (Braesemann and Graham, 2020).

These trends have had myriad outcomes. Advocates argue that these flows have created much-needed employment opportunities and supported economic diversification, promoted FDI flows, and boosted economic growth in many countries. However, critics highlight how such flows have also decimated existing employment markets and resulted in unemployment (for instance, the South African textile industry has been largely destroyed in the face of cheap imports from China), have resulted in exploitative working conditions (particularly in the garment and technology sectors), support continued extraction of resources (and profits) to global elites and TNCs/MNCs headquartered in the global north, contribute to environment degradation and damage in the global south, and, linked to this, have made everyday life more insecure for many (in particular, human and environmental rights defenders).

EXPORT PROCESSING AND FREE TRADE ZONES

The processes integral to the NIDL have combined with efforts by various governments to encourage FDI and entice MNCs to (re) locate activities to their countries through the creation of 'Export Processing Zones' (EPZs), Free Trade Zones (FTZs), and use of other investment spaces and policies. EPZs are specially designated spaces that benefit from tax breaks and other subsidies for international corporations and investors. States establish EPZs in the hope of gaining a 'comparative advantage' and attract FDI and MNCs/ TNCs to set up operations in these spaces based upon the potential for these companies to generate increased profits through a combination of lower taxes and overheads, few (if any) legal protections for workers, and the availability of low-paid and flexible labour.

For the host countries, EPZs and FTZs may provide a much-needed boost to national economies via FDI, job creation, and investments in and improvements to infrastructure and knowledge. These spaces are often also credited with creating new work opportunities for (young) women, although these opportunities can lead to a growing set of demands on women who are expected (by social norms) to continue providing their unpaid reproductive labour (caring roles, running households, etc.). Furthermore, claims about employment creation by EPZs are subject to challenge: Are these jobs 'new' or just 'alternative' to or resulting from the loss of other jobs?

EPZs and FTZs are thus often seen as bringing limited tangible benefit to the host country. Yes, there may be an increase in certain forms of employment and thus the potential for increased circulation of money within the local economy. However, these inflows are offset by the retention of power – and profits – by major corporations and declining working and environmental conditions. For decades we have witnessed campaigns against 'sweatshop' labour and calls for improvements in the working conditions in companies' supply chains. Yet progress is negligible at best: while writing this book, the fast-fashion brand Shein were engulfed in scandal when it was revealed that their suppliers were paying workers as little as 3p per item made, with staff working 18-hour shifts to earn $3, with only one day off per month. Elsewhere, we see repeated concerns raised over working conditions in factories producing components, assembled products, or clothing for companies including Apple, Marks and Spencer, Boohoo, Hewlett Packard, and others. These workforces are often predominantly female (often also young and unmarried) due to employers seeking out cheap and dexterous staff who are seen as less likely to be disruptive. Data from the ILO indicate that 95% of workers in EPZs in Panama were women, while 80% of workers in Guatemalan and Nicaraguan EPZs were women. Layered onto concerns with low wages and poor working conditions, the lack of protections for women in these sectors means they are at heightened vulnerability for (sexual) harassment and abuse, as well as experiencing discrimination against pregnant women and a lack of maternity leave.

Elsewhere, we see the everyday (violent) realities facing trade union, human rights, and environmental activists who seek to challenge corporations and protect communities and the environment. In 2022 alone we saw reports of intimidation, forced disappearances, and murders of Indigenous community activists and advocates (including Bruno Pereira and Dom Phillips in Brazil), environmental and land defenders (Bolivia, Paraguay), and human rights activists and trade unionists (Cameroon, Cuba, Dominican Republic). According to the human rights organisation Front Line Defenders (2022), 358 human rights defenders were killed across 35 countries in 2021 – 138 of whom were killed in Colombia, 42 in Mexico, 27 in Brazil, and 23 in India – with thousands of further reports of arrests, detentions, surveillance, threats, beatings, legal action, and other violations. Across the last decade, Global Witness (2022) reports more than 1,700 killings of environmental and land defenders (that's one killing every other day), with Indigenous communities particularly targeted (Indigenous communities account for 5% of the global population, but 40% of attacks on environmental and land defenders).

GLOBALISATION'S GENDERED IMPACT

Globalisation's impact on women – and on gender relations – has been varied. Increased flows of ideas and expanding solidarity and activist networks have promoted social change, women's rights, and challenged patriarchal norms (with varying levels of success). Flows of cultural information and media influences, including the spread of 'Western' lifestyles and values, as well as reactions against these influences, have contributed to changing understandings of and engagements with gender roles and identities.

Economic growth and the NIDL have contributed to an increased role for women in the labour market: in 1990 women earned 30% of global labour income; by 2020 this had risen to 35% (Chancel et al., 2022). While this may, on the face of it, seem a positive trend, critics caution that the feminisation of the labour force has varied outcomes and impacts as these changes have – at times – come into tension with established social and cultural expectations and norms. According to the ILO (2022a), 94.6% of men globally participate in the labour market compared with 51.6% of women. Whereas the participation rate for men stays relatively constant regardless of household type, for women it varies dramatically: from 82.4% of women living alone to 41.1% for women in extended families with a child under 6 years old. In addition, there are considerable gendered variations in labour market participation by region (Figure 4.1).

In some contexts the increase in share of global labour income has correlated with decreasing gender pay gaps, improved working conditions and protections for female workers, and efforts to tackle gender discrimination and the 'glass ceiling'. However, such progress is far from universal. While the global gender pay gap may be reducing (to 11% in 2022 (ILO, 2022b)), huge variations exist: for instance, in Ghana the pay gap was 64%, in Rwanda 40%, Sierra Leone 38%, and Liberia 35%.

In many contexts the growth in employment opportunities for women has been marked by job insecurity, low pay, harassment, exploitation, and social stigma. Societies and social norms have not always kept pace with the increasing role of women in the labour

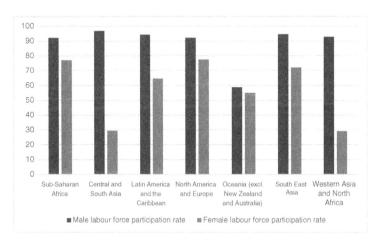

Figure 4.1 Regional labour market participation rates by gender
Source: Compiled from data from ILO (2022a)

market. In some situations, the challenge to or reversal of traditional gender roles (the male 'breadwinner' and female 'homemaker') has challenged ideas of femininity and masculinity. This unsettling of traditional norms has been linked to various experiences of changing gender relations: from increases in gender-based violence and a rise in mental health and substance abuse issues amongst men whose sense of (masculine) identity has been challenged, to rising divorce rates and greater independence of women who no longer feel reliant upon a male breadwinner. Elsewhere, the feminisation of the labour market has led to increases in the expectations and burdens on women who face pressures to both earn an income while continuing to run the household. Thus, while women (in general) are undertaking increasing amounts of paid work, this is not resulting in a proportionate decrease in unpaid work. As Azcona and Bhatt (2019) outline, women undertake (on average) 272 minutes of unpaid or care work per day (the reproductive labour of running a household and caring for children and other family members), compared to 84 minutes for men. Meanwhile men spend 321 minutes on paid work, compared to 181 minutes for women, meaning the overall time spent on work by women is significantly higher: 454 minutes compared with 405 minutes for men.

Experiences of migration have also been gendered, from the 'trailing spouses' of highly skilled, footloose migrants to the gendered flows (particularly in Asia) of women seeking work as domestic workers, care workers, and in informal sectors. Much of this migration is driven by financial need and pressures to diversify or find alternative household income streams to support families. While these flows can provide essential income and remittances, these moves come with significant risk and vulnerabilities as well as separation from loved ones. These migrations also have implications for those left behind – grandparents and other relatives who take on additional caring responsibilities, children whose parent(s) undertake labour migration – and lead to the growth of a 'care deficit'.

TRADE FLOWS

As mentioned earlier, trade has been integral to globalisation – including in the pre-colonial and colonial eras. Given the volume of trade flows each year, trade clearly has huge potential to promote and support global development. According to UNCTAD (UN Conference on Trade and Development), in 2021 global trade in both goods and services was valued at $28.5 trillion ($28,500,000,000,000), with particular growth in the value of exports from the global south and south–south trade. This increase was linked, in part at least, to rises in commodity values – resulting in increased revenues for commodity-exporting countries (UNCTAD, 2022a). Between 2018 and 2021, exports from least developed countries grew from $240 billion (comprised of $200 billion in goods exports and $40 billion of services) to $258 billion (of which, goods accounted for $229 billion, compared to $29 billion for services) (WTO, 2022). As history has demonstrated, however, trade relations can also function to entrench inequalities, support resource extractivism, and maintain the wealth and power of the global north. Indeed, the dominance of manufacturing exports by China (15% of the global total), the US (8%), and Germany (7%), as well as Asia and Europe's ascendancy in production and export of intermediate goods (things like semiconductors, pharma ingredients, etc. that are used in supply chains), indicate the continued skewing of global trade relations (WTO, 2022).

Compounding these imbalances, the precarity of the growth in trade and exports for least developed countries (and other commodity-dependent economies) is reflected in UNCTAD's *Trade and Development Report 2022* (UNCTAD, 2022b). This report cautions that monetary policy decisions in the global north risk stimulating a global recession and economic instability to a worse degree than the 2008 financial crisis. Such an eventuality would reduce trade flows and trigger reductions or collapses in commodity markets, while decisions by governments to increase interest rates will further compound matters (for instance, interest rate rises in the US in 2022 are expected to reduce income for the global south by $360 billion (UNCTAD, 2022b)). These risks come on top of the disruptions to trade flows and fluctuations in commodity prices in recent years – from the disruption to supply chains and trade during the Covid-19 pandemic, to the effects of the Russian invasion of Ukraine in 2022 which has led to a significant decrease in the value of imports to and exports from the Commonwealth of Independent States region, as well as spikes in energy and food prices.

Other key factors that influence the potential for trade to support global development include protectionist policies that are used to increase the costs of imports while protecting domestic producers. In simple terms, these are commonly encountered in three ways: as subsidies for domestic producers (this is where a government provides financial support to growers, producers, and manufacturers to keep prices lower while boosting profit margins), import quotas (which limit how much of a product can be imported), and both tariff and non-tariff barriers (tariffs are the costs imposed on imported products; non-tariff barriers being quality standards or other regulatory requirements).

Subsidies are used to support producers, exporters, and consumers in different ways but with the same common objective: to promote economic growth and productivity. This can be in the form of production subsidies (to encourage certain production activities, from agriculture to manufacturing), consumption subsidies (offsetting costs of food, water, energy, etc.), and export subsidies (offsetting costs of exports). However, while these measures may support economic growth they can also distort prices and markets, which can in turn lead to global tensions and 'trade wars'. The use of agricultural subsidies by North American and European countries has long been viewed as an unfair intervention in markets by countries in the global south. In this situation, the subsidising of production costs for agricultural goods in the global north undercuts or suppresses the value of products from other countries. At the same time, the use of tariffs and other barriers further increases the costs of imports in order to support domestic producers and economies.

In general terms, tariffs are levied on imported products to raise revenue for government but are used to offer protection to domestic industry by increasing the costs of imported goods. One way in which this is done is through escalating tariffs linked to the level of processing of a product: a raw material (cocoa, coffee, etc.) would incur very low tariffs, whereas a processed product (chocolate) would incur a higher charge. This differential cost means many countries in the global south continue to rely upon primary commodity exports, rather than processed goods.

Complicating the picture, not all countries are treated equally. We see groups of countries entering into 'regional' or 'preferential' trade agreements such as the North Atlantic Free Trade Agreement (NAFTA), the European Free Trade Area (EFTA), Mercado Comun del Cono Sur or Southern Common Market (MERCOSUR), and many others (there were over 280 trading agreements in place in 2017 (World Bank, 2022)). These agreements reduce or remove tariffs and/or other barriers on trade between states who are part of the agreement. Typically, these agreements perpetuate particular forms of relations and continue to exclude countries from the global south, resulting in higher costs and other barriers to exports from these countries to major economies in the global north.

MIGRATION AND FLOWS OF PEOPLE, SKILLS, AND KNOWLEDGE

Alongside the growth in financial flows linked to globalisation, we have witnessed increasing flows of people around the world. Over the past 50 years there has been a 300% increase in international migration flows, with millions of people moving across national borders each year. These movements incorporate a vast array of migrant groups – from ultra-high net worth individuals through high-skilled and other elite migrants to (temporary and circular) labour migrants, refugees, asylum seekers, and 'illegal' migrants.

By mid-2020, the International Organization for Migration (IOM) estimated that there were 281 million international migrants around the world, including 164 million migrant workers, with international migrants and diasporas responsible for transferring $702 billion in remittances (IOM, 2022). International migration intersects with global development concerns on multiple levels, beginning with the drivers of migration. People migrate for a whole variety of reasons: to reunite with family; in search of work, economic opportunities, and a better quality of life; to escape violence, persecution, and conflict; or due to the impacts of climate change and natural hazards. Some may intend to migrate on a short-term basis, others on a long-term basis, and others on a circular basis (e.g. seasonal agricultural work). Some migrants are encouraged or welcomed by recipient state governments (typically wealthy or skilled individuals, especially those from states in the global north), whereas others are demonised and detained (primarily those with limited financial capital, few qualifications, or travelling from countries in the global south).

Globalisation is linked to an increasing differentiation in mobility: increased freedom of movement for privileged elites (and financial capital) contrasting with increasing barriers to movement for those depicted as 'undesirable'. These processes are reflected in the contrast between the ability of the (ultra-)wealthy to use their financial capital to secure residence or citizenship through investments (so-called 'golden passport' or investor citizenship schemes) in various countries, and the use of offshore and external detention for refugees and asylum seekers by Australia and other nations.

In recent years, the potential global development benefits of migration have increasingly focused on the role of migrants and diasporas in supporting development 'back home' through remittance flows. This focus on remittances has followed previous concerns around the impacts of skilled migration from, typically, poorer states to richer ones. Dubbed 'brain drain', this process remains a critical concern to many, as skilled workers – doctors, nurses, scientists, and others – migrate overseas in search of higher pay, improved working conditions and career opportunities, and a better quality of life. Compounding this concern, many countries in the global north have relied upon these flows of skilled workers to fill job vacancies without incurring the costs of training these workers. Given the heavily gendered nature of migration of emotional and care labour from the global south to the global north, commentators have referred to the emergence of 'global care chains'. This concept refers to the practices through which countries in the global north target workers from the global south to fill shortages in labour markets while leaving the 'costs' of the reproduction of this labour force to the sending countries. Examples of this abound, and we need look no further than active efforts by the UK's National Health Service over many years to recruit healthcare professionals from across the world.

While concerns with the dangers of 'brain drain' remain, particularly for conflict-affected and least developed countries, there is growing recognition that these migration flows may also provide benefits – in the form of remittances, but also in the potential for 'brain circulation' (the return migration of those who move overseas but then return home, potentially with further training, knowledge, and skills) and the flows of student migration.

Alongside these forms of 'skilled migration', movements of 'un-' or 'low'-skilled migrants must be recognised. Whether as seasonal agricultural workers (for example, Mexican workers travelling to

California, or Eastern European workers on fruit and vegetable farms in England), construction workers (as to Qatar in the lead-up to the 2022 FIFA World Cup), or domestic and care workers (such as to Singapore), millions of people move each year. These flows are vital not only for the businesses and economies dependent upon their labour, but also for those gaining employment and their families. However, these migrants are often in more precarious and vulnerable positions, at risk from poor working conditions, of sexual or other abuse, the unfair/illegal withholding of pay by unscrupulous employers, and with limited rights and protections.

There exists an even darker side to migration: human trafficking, forced labour, and modern slavery. These are global issues, with forced labour and modern slavery implicated in numerous industries including fishing, agriculture, mining, garments, domestic work, electronics, and beyond. There are estimated to be over 21 million victims, with companies and organised crime generating over $150 billion a year in illegal profits from the labour of these victims (LeBaron, 2016). At the same time, we are seeing expansion of people smuggling and human trafficking organisations, including the 'coyotes' operating on the US/Mexico border, criminal gangs operating smuggling routes into Europe, and organisations trafficking men, women, and children around the world. Tracking thousands of cases, the CT Data Collaborative (CTDC) has noted increasing levels of trafficking, in particular of female victims (especially girls). Noting regional variations in human trafficking, CTDC (2022) identifies that victims are primarily trafficked for domestic work in Asia, for sexual exploitation in the Americas (where 80% of victims are female), and for both labour and sexual exploitation in Europe.

INTERNAL MIGRATION

While the focus of attention in popular discussions of migration tends to dwell upon international migration, a key factor in global development is also internal (or intra-national) migration. Most commonly this is experienced as rural-to-urban movement (typically of younger people seeking access to education or employment opportunities), but also includes urban-to-rural, rural-to-rural, and urban-to-urban flows. These movements can have profound development impacts, from the 'hollowing out' of working-age populations in rural communities to the pressures on housing and land access and tenure, service delivery, and governance structures in rapidly expanding urban areas.

In rural areas, high levels of emigration can create key challenges including grandparent and child-headed households, challenges in recruiting professionals (especially in health-care and education) to deliver key services in rural areas, and economic stagnation. On the flip side, these migration flows can be essential household livelihood diversification strategies, with internal remittances (from the urban migrant to their rural 'home') providing a vital household income stream. In urban areas, challenges arising from in-migration can include shortages of housing and land, lack of basic service delivery, and competition for employment and other resources – including control over local or street-level politics.

LAND GRABS, LAND TENURE, AND RURAL DEVELOPMENT

While the world's population is increasingly urbanised, rural poverty and development remain crucial – not least as poverty rates in rural areas are often higher than in urban spaces. Poverty in rural areas is complex and can often be compounded by the migration of younger and working-age residents to urban areas in search of employment and life opportunities. Extreme poverty rates thus vary from 5.5% for women and 5.4% for men in urban spaces to 19% for women and 18.1% for men in rural areas (Azcona and Bhatt, 2019).

Key factors in rural poverty and livelihoods include issues of (gendered) land access and tenure, marginal profits on crops and the balancing of growing subsistence crops or crops for sale (either at local markets or for export), limited and unreliable infrastructure, increased transportation costs, increasing risks of lost income from crop failures or natural hazards, and so on. During the 1960s, rural development agendas were heavily informed by the 'Green Revolution'. Based upon successful projects in Asia, the Green Revolution was adopted more widely in an effort to promote rural economic growth and poverty reduction. This aim of this 'revolution' was to enable rural farmers to increase their crop yields and profits, generating a self-reinforcing cycle of prosperity and growth. To do this, farmers would purchase new (more resilient and higher-yielding) seed varieties, increased fertiliser inputs, and technological solutions to boost yields and profits. Those able to afford these increased input costs were able to reap the benefits. However, this also resulted in increased dependency on imported inputs, expertise, and technology while also exacerbating rural inequalities.

Following the Green Revolution, thinking about rural development and livelihoods turned to the work of Robert Chambers and his thinking on capabilities, social and material assets, activities, and the importance of different forms of capital and networks to support livelihoods. This work gave rise to the livelihoods approach to rural development which focuses on empowering rural households to make decisions about and enhance their ability to access and use different assets, resources, and forms of capital – from natural capital such as land and water, through physical capital (energy, food, transport, equipment) and human capital (labour, skills) to social (trust, reciprocity, networks) and economic capital (income, savings, etc.). Linked to this thinking, various development strategies have sought to encourage and strengthen livelihood diversification in households to reduce dependency on (and thus risks linked to) single income sources, including through diversification of crops/livestock, development of micro-businesses, and household migration strategies.

As noted earlier, one key factor for rural development is land: Who has access to and/or ownership of land? How is access managed and governed? These concerns are crucial for households reliant upon agriculture as a livelihood strategy, particularly when access is potentially jeopardised or is contested due to differing livelihood strategies. For instance, tensions emerge between pastoralist and agriculturalist livelihoods in the West Pokot region of Kenya. Here, differing livelihood approaches come into tension as pastoralist herders move their livestock in search of food and water, potentially coming onto farmed land and damaging crops. Such conflicts can be long-running and, on occasion, can have fatal consequences.

Pressures on land – in particular for subsistence farming – arise from the expansion of export agriculture. In many regions of the world, smallholder farmers are encouraged to grow crops for export markets (thereby reducing production for household use or local markets) or vast amounts of land are purchased by commercial companies (and even other states) specifically to grow crops for export. This can lead to extensive monocropping (growing of a single crop) – for instance, roses in Kenya, green beans in Egypt – predestined for sale and consumption in the global north. Leaving aside the carbon footprint of these practices, other local impacts include loss of land for local growers, increased use of chemicals to support commercial farming which often leads to pollution of local lakes and water supplies, and the (unsustainable) exploitation of water resources. As we look towards an increasingly insecure climate future amid rising concerns over food security, competition over land (and the acquisition and use of land by parastatals and foreign governments) will become an increasing concern.

This concern is exacerbated by growing awareness of the negative impacts of land degradation: in 2022, the destruction of the Amazon rainforest had reached the point where it has ceased to be a carbon sink and is now a net emitter of carbon. It is estimated that 12 million hectares of farmland (that's 16.8 million football pitches, or the equivalent of North Korea) becomes unusable each year, whether due to desertification, depletion of nutrients in soils, or other factors (UN, 2019). Overall, agricultural practices worldwide account for between 19% and 29% of greenhouse emissions – from burning of forests for ranching or farming, the methane produced by livestock, and other activities.

Further pressures on land have arisen from the growing global demand for biofuels in the 2000s. Seen by techno-optimists as a key solution to climate change and fossil fuel dependency, there was a rush to embrace biofuels as a green energy source. In 2013, 41.3 million hectares of land (approximately 4% of available arable land) and 216 billion cubic metres of water were used to produce 86 million tons of biofuels (Rulli et al., 2016). It is estimated that this land could have been used to grow crops to feed 30% of those who are malnourished worldwide (Rulli et al., 2016). This shift to using biomass (from sugary or starchy crops (bioethanol) and fats and plant oils (biodiesel)) as an alternative to fossil fuels may help reduce carbon emissions, but this comes at a cost. There has been a rash of large-scale commercial land grabs and both the repurposing of land use away from food production and the destruction of forests and other environments to accommodate this new crop. These land purchases were typically focussed in equatorial regions, leading to large-scale land dispossession, livelihood insecurities, as well as both local and global food price rises (Smith, 2010).

A key limitation of many approaches to rural development has been a failure to adequately engage with gender. Women have often been overlooked in relation to (re)productive labour in rural communities, including in agriculture but also household decision making and management. Additionally, interventions have often failed to adequately consider how women often have less stable access to (smaller) plots of land, have greater household labour burdens (collecting water, firewood, cooking, cleaning, childcare), face greater barriers to education, and may have more limited assets to use to pay for inputs to crops. Compounding these concerns, women may also be excluded from inheritance and other cultural and social norms which further marginalise women in various ways. Recent years have seen various efforts to target rural women – through microcredit schemes, entrepreneurial training projects, and efforts to tackle structural barriers around inheritance and land rights, as well as broader national policies such as (un) conditional cash transfers (UCTs and CCTs) focused on supporting (in particular, girls') access to health care and education via the transfer of social grant funds to female household members.

(UN)CONDITIONAL CASH TRANSFERS

Approaches to supporting development and poverty reduction have included microcredit and microfinance, as well as savings collectives; social protection has also emerged as a key poverty reduction mechanism. These practices include state pensions, child support grants, (Universal) Basic Income Grants, and other forms of unconditional and conditional cash transfers.

Two increasingly common approaches to welfare support are conditional and unconditional cash transfers (CCTs and UCTs). Sitting alongside 'supply-side' provision of education and healthcare funding, this 'demand-side' approach seeks to influence and change individual behaviour. In so doing, CCT and UCT programmes provide poor families with money directly from the government – in essence, a form of social welfare payment: for example, Ghana's Livelihood Empowerment Against Poverty (LEAP) 1000 programme for pregnant women and new mothers; Malawi's Social Cash Transfer Program; Zambia's Child Grant Program (CGP) and Multiple Category Targeted Program (MCP); and Mexico's Progresa (now Prospera) programme.

By far the more common approach are CCTs – where money is provided to families in return for certain behavioural change. The first generation of these programmes emerged in the 1990s, spreading from Brazil and Mexico to countries across the world including Honduras, Jamaica, Turkey, Nicaragua, and beyond. Designed to meet immediate financial needs and poverty alleviation while tackling the root causes of intergenerational poverty, CCTs have provided effective mechanisms for reaching the poor and promoting longer-term human capital accumulation (Rasella et al., 2013; Rawlings and Rubio, 2005). These programmes generally focus on children as beneficiaries – by promoting the health and education of young people, it is hoped that this will break intergenerational poverty cycles. Hence, typical conditionalities for cash transfers will require certain levels of attendance at school over a defined time period or compliance with required attendance at health clinics and vaccinations. Typically, mothers are usually the designated recipients of the cash transfers in recognition of their role in household decision making.

Unconditional cash transfers, as the name suggests, are social protection payments made to poor and vulnerable groups without any requirement for behaviour change or compliance. These are implemented in various forms, including universal basic income. Generally, UCTs are seen as likely having positive effects on ensuring household food security, reducing levels of extreme poverty, improving health, and increasing school enrolment.

Some critics have argued that it would be more appropriate to provide in-kind support or payments in the form of vouchers that can be redeemed in particular shops or for particular types of goods only. Advocates of these more restrictive forms of provision argue that this prevents recipients spending the payments on 'luxury' goods such as alcohol or entertainment. However, such an approach is increasingly recognised as demeaning and paternalistic, stripping the agency and decision-making independence of the poor, while also leading to unintended price distortions in the market. Monitoring and evaluation evidence of multiple CCT programmes has shown positive outcomes not only in education attendance and health visits, but also in improvements to diets and increased spending on fruits, vegetables, and animal products – although it should also be noted that CCTs are also linked to increases in consumption levels of sugar and rising rates of obesity and hypertension. UCTs can also enhance levels of social participation and engagement, supporting further reciprocal support networks and leading to improvements in both economic and emotional well-being and mental health.

INFORMAL AND SHADOW ECONOMIES

Alongside efforts to promote formal economic growth and policy efforts to support poor families through CCTs and UCTs, another key area of economic activity remains vital for livelihoods in many contexts: the informal or shadow economy.

What do we mean by the informal and shadow economies? In simple terms, these are economic activities that are hidden, avoiding the gaze of the tax-office and other state oversight. The sector comprises a vast range of activities including undeclared second jobs, cash-in-hand work, clandestine and illicit work (including drug dealing and arms smuggling), as well as work by illegal immigrants. In other words, 'those economic activities and the income derived from them that circumvent or otherwise avoid government regulation, taxation or observation' (Schneider, 2016: 187).

By its very hidden nature, it is notoriously difficult to accurately estimate the size of the informal economy: needless to say, it is significant! OECD data (reported in Schneider, 2016) from the early 2000s suggest that over 50% of agricultural jobs in the global south and 80% of non-agricultural jobs in sub-Saharan Africa and South Asia are 'informal'. This is not to say that the informal economy is restricted to countries in the global south – it is estimated that the informal economy is worth 13.4% of national GDP in countries in the OECD, a figure rising to 37.6% in sub-Saharan Africa and 34.7% in Latin America and the Caribbean (Schneider, 2016: 191).

Rather than viewing the informal or shadow economy as an outlier or abnormality it is important to recognise that it is ubiquitous – and a key livelihood strategy for millions. In many regions it provides a vital means of income and livelihood generation – from artisanal mining or manufacturing, through street trading, to off-the-books educational tutoring or seasonal agricultural work – as well as flexibility to work at times, in locations, and in ways that can fit more flexibly to individual circumstance. Other drivers to participation in the informal economy include a lack of available (and appropriate) employment in the formal sector, and individuals avoiding the increased administration burden of formal reporting (which can also include considerations of language and literacy), as well as distrust in local or state authorities. Meanwhile, critics argue that the failure to collect taxes on these earnings is a major cost to national treasuries and that those working in the sector suffer greater precarity, lower pay, poorer working conditions, and a lack of protections.

FINANCING DEVELOPMENT – TAXATION

Other key finance concerns in relation to global development include the role of taxation. Taxes are crucial for governments, providing the revenue through which debts are paid off, public sector and civil servant salaries are paid, and development projects, infrastructure, and services are paid for. Clear, effective, and robust tax regimes can support state legitimacy and can be used to strategically support poverty reduction, investment to support productivity, and promote development outcomes. However, multiple challenges remain – from issues with corruption and tax avoidance and evasion, through to the use of tax havens, and questions of where transnational/multinational corporations pay taxes. Governments also come under intense political pressures – on one side from those demanding progressive taxes to promote social justice and reduce inequalities (often dubbed 'pro-poor'), and on the other from those advocating for lower taxes as a means of promoting business and investment ('pro-market'). Regardless of the tax agenda adopted, all governments need tax revenues to function and failure to collect these revenues (so-called 'lost tax') can undermine development agendas.

The challenge of lost taxes is enormous. The State of Tax Justice Report (Cobham et al., 2020) estimates that $427 billion of taxes are 'lost' globally each year: that's the equivalent of South Africa's entire GDP, or almost 2.5 times the total amount of ODA flows. Of this $427 billion in lost taxes, $245 billion is linked to MNCs' use of tax havens and $182 billion to wealthy individuals avoiding taxes through offshore banking and investments. While the amount lost is much higher for EMDCs ($382.7 billion) than for ELDCs ($45 billion), the proportional impact on ELDCs is much higher at 5.8% of tax revenues (compared to 2.5% of tax revenues in EMDCs) and is the equivalent of almost 52% of their health budgets. If these numbers seem a little off-putting, the State of Tax Justice Report (Cobham et al., 2020) offers a more accessible way of thinking about the relative costs of these losses for each country by translating the lost taxes into the number of nurses this lost revenue could pay for (see Table 4.1). This disproportionate impact is further exacerbated as those experiencing the biggest impact of the loss of investment and funding from tax avoidance and evasion are the poor and marginalised: those who often not only rely more directly on social services and welfare, but who also pick up the burden of care when these services are lacking.

Table 4.1 Tax revenue losses for selected countries

Country	Tax revenue loss (US$)	Tax loss as % of collected tax revenue	Tax loss as # of nurses' salaries
Colombia	11,774,915,838	18.2	2,465,001
India	10,319,683,940	0.41	4,230,656
Mexico	9,067,461,243	6.45	581,552
Netherlands	10,601,294,005	5.43	160,902
Nigeria	10,825,786,952	2.4	3,532,455
South Africa	3,391,890,587	3.43	1,068,770
Sudan	7,247,646	30.37	423,342
UK	39,583,847,405	5.35	840,209
Vietnam	420,826,698	0.98	121,329

Source: State of Tax Justice Report (Cobham et al., 2020: 28–33)

Complicating this issue is the role of the informal and shadow economies. The scale of the informal economy (discussed earlier) means many view this as a vital, untapped revenue stream for governments. But how do you try to capture a largely hidden and cash-based set of economic practices? In other words, how do you formalise the informal economy? While Ghana has brought in some innovative policies to begin to do this, key challenges remain as efforts to formalise the informal sector may actually result in a decline in economic activity and growth in unemployment and poverty. Efforts to formalise the informal economy are also highly contentious and often politicised: in Uganda, for instance, the street-level governance and power of various informal economy collectives (such as the boda-boda (motorbike taxi) drivers) are courted by politicians to mobilise support in elections. As a result, efforts to regulate and tax this sector would be – to say the least – complicated. There are contrasting schools of thought on formalising the informal sector: some argue the informal sector is an integral and vital livelihood space, with any effort to formalise resulting in deepening inequalities and poverty; whereas advocates for formalisation point to the need for regulation and worker protections, and to collect lost taxes in order to support development spending and reduce national debt.

NATIONAL DEBT

The issue of national (foreign) debt is seen by many as key to sustainable development. Foreign debt is the amount owed to overseas (foreign) lenders/creditors, typically in 'hard' currencies such as the US dollar, Euros, or British pound. These debts are due to different types of lenders including national governments, state-owned banks, private banks, and international financial institutions. Why do governments borrow money, you might be thinking? Why not just print more of it? The simplified answer is that if a government printed more and more money this would lead to the devaluation of the currency – in other words, it would become worth less and less, driving up prices and inflation and destabilising the economy. To avoid this, governments borrow from lenders to cover their spending – be this on health, education, infrastructure, or other costs – which exceeds their income (tax revenue). This may be done to meet temporary shortfalls in tax payments, investment in major and expensive (development) projects, or in the face of unexpected costs (such as conflict or the Covid-19 pandemic).

Virtually all governments have a national debt – in 2022 the UK national debt was £2,365 billion (99.6% of GDP), the US's stood at $30.93 trillion (124% of GDP), and India's $620.7 million (84% of GDP), whereas China's 2021 debt was $3,651 billion (20.3% of GDP). For many countries in the global south, levels of national debt and repayment costs are key hindrances to national development and economic growth.

The burden of debt repayments can be highlighted by considering what percentage of government revenue each country is spending on national debts, and how this varies between states. Thus, while many global north states have extensive national debts their 'service payments' are often relatively low; for instance, countries such as Sweden, Denmark, the UK, Israel, and Japan spend between 1% and 4% of revenues on debt. Meanwhile, many states in the global south face much higher debt costs as a percentage of government income: the People's Republic of Lao debt payments account for 31.1% of government revenue, for Gabon this figure is 59.5%, for Ghana it is 50.2%, for Bhutan it is 49%, in Lebanon it is 40.3%, and – at the extreme – for Venezuela this figure is an entirely unsustainable 266.4% (Jubilee Debt Campaign, 2021). Even in countries with relatively low levels of debt servicing payments, these costs are still used in arguments to reduce public spending and usher in 'austerity' policies – as we have seen in the UK and elsewhere.

Given the high levels of debt servicing costs for many countries, it is unsurprising that we hear talk of countries being in 'debt distress', in 'danger of defaulting on repayments', or even 'going bankrupt'. In 2021, the IMF identified 9 countries as have stopped repaying their external debts (being in 'debt distress') with a further 28 countries at high risk of defaulting on repayments. In the same year, and using different criteria, the Jubilee Debt Campaign (2021) identified 52 countries (over 25% of the world's countries) as being in debt crisis – defined as being where 'debt payments undermine a country's economy and/or the ability of its government to protect the basic economic and social rights of its citizens', with a further 63 countries being at risk of debt crisis.

Driving these fears are combinations of rising interest rates and inflation, the global energy crisis and rising costs of living, as well as the economic impacts of climate change (in terms of both disruptions to food production as well as the costs of floods and other hazards) and Covid-19. These pressures mean that much of the progress of the early 2000s in reducing external debts is being undone. In 1998 the cost of debt servicing payments for impoverished countries stood (on average) at 16.6% of government revenue. By 2011 this figure had dropped to an average of 5.5% of government revenue due to a combination of increased trade revenue (due to commodity price increases) and debt relief through the Heavily Indebted Poor Countries Initiative and Multilateral Debt Relief Initiative (Jubilee Debt Campaign, 2020: 3).

However, there has been a reversal of this trend since 2011 – with debt repayments for impoverished countries rising to 12.4% of government revenue in 2019. In simple terms, this means that indebted countries – in particular, heavily indebted countries – are having to spend increasing amounts of their tax revenue on debt repayments and interest, meaning there is less available to spend on health, education, welfare, infrastructure, and other national priorities. As the Jubilee Debt Campaign's research shows, these costs are reflected in the decrease of 6% in public spending per person in the countries with the highest debt payments while those with the lowest repayments have seen an average increase of 14% in public spending (Jubilee Debt Campaign, 2020).

Consequently, the Jubilee Debt Campaign and others argue that major lenders should write-off (drop) the debts owed by countries in the global south. Arguments for 'drop the debt' included recognition that many debts have been inherited from previous rulers and may have been contracted unfairly or undemocratically – for instance, a debt may have been taken on to pay for military costs to retain authoritarian power. Second, the repayments required on debts (and the interest accrued) can often be unsustainable, requiring governments to reduce spending on health, education, and social services and/or to take out new debts to pay back old debts.

These challenges are not new: the 1980s witnessed a global debt crisis as debtor nations struggled to repay high-interest loans taken out in the 1970s to promote industrialisation-led development.

Repayments rapidly became unsustainable in the face of rising oil prices, a stalling of the world economy, and collapse in primary commodity markets (which were the main source of revenue for many debtor countries). Facing declining trade revenues and foreign direct investment, many countries in the global south sought support from the World Bank and IMF.

REFERENCES

Azcona, G., Bhatt, A. (2019). Understanding gender differences in poverty: A global snapshot. New York: UN Women. https://unece.org/fileadmin/DAM/stats/documents/ece/ces/ge.15/2019/mtg2/PPP_2_UN_Women.pdf (retrieved 04/01/2023).

Bakker, K. (2013). Constructing 'public' water: The World Bank, urban water supply, and the biopolitics of development. *Environment and Planning D: Society and Space*, 31 (2): 280–300.

Belaid, F., Dagher, L., Filis, G. (2021). Revisiting the resource curse in the MENA region. *Resources Policy*, 73: 102225.

Benería, L., Berik, G., Floro, M.S. (2016). *Gender, Development and Globalization: Economics as if All People Mattered*. Abingdon: Routledge.

Braesemann, F., Graham, M. (2020). Understanding the global geography of platform work. In *32nd Annual Meeting*, 18–21 July 2020 (virtual conference). Society for the Advancement of Socio-Economics.

Carmody, P. (2008). Exploring Africa's economic recovery. *Geography Compass*, 2 (1): 79–107.

Chancel, L., Piketty, T., Saez, E., Zucman, G. (2022). *World Inequality Report 2022*. Paris: World Inequality Lab, UNDP.

Cobham, A., Garcia-Bernardo, J., Palansky, M., Mansour, M.B. (2020). *The State of Tax Justice Report 2020: Tax Justice in the time of COVID-19*. Bristol: Tax Justice Network. https://taxjustice.net/reports/the-state-of-tax-justice-2020/ (retrieved 20/02/2023).

CTDC (2022). Global data hub on human trafficking. Geneva: International Organization for Migration. https://www.ctdatacollaborative.org/ (retrieved 07/12/2022).

Front Line Defenders (2022). Global analysis 2021. Dublin: Front Line Defenders. https://www.frontlinedefenders.org/en/resource-publication/global-analysis-2021-0 (retrieved 09/12/2022).

Global Witness (2022). A deadly decade for land and environmental activists – with a killing every two days. London: Global Witness. https://www.globalwitness.org/en/press-releases/deadly-decade-land-and-environmental-activists-killing-every-two-days/ (retrieved 09/12/2022).

Goldin, I. (2018). *Development: A Very Short Introduction*. Oxford: Oxford University Press.

Haarstad, H. (2016). Natural resource extraction and the development conundrum. In Grugel, J., Hammett, D. (eds) *The Palgrave Handbook of International Development* (pp. 139–154). London: Palgrave Macmillan.

Harrison, G. (2010). *Neoliberal Africa: The Impact of Global Social Engineering*. London: Zed Books.

Hickel, J. (2021). What does degrowth mean? A few points of clarification. *Globalizations*, 18 (7): 1105–1111.

ILO (2022a). Statistics on Women. Geneva: International Labour Organization. https://ilostat.ilo.org/topics/women/ (retrieved 04/01/2023).

ILO (2022b). Labour statistics for the Sustainable Development Goals (SDGs). Geneva: International Labour Organization. https://ilostat.ilo.org/topics/sdg/ (retrieved 04/01/2023).

IOM (2022). Data and research. Geneva: International Organization for Migration. https://www.iom.int/data-and-research (retrieved 09/12/2022).

Jubilee Debt Campaign (2020). The growing global south debt crisis and cuts in public spending. London: Jubilee Debt Campaign. https://jubileedebt. org.uk/wp-content/uploads/2020/01/The-growing-global-South-debt-crisis-and-cuts-in-public-spending_01.20.pdf (retrieved 14/06/2022).

Jubilee Debt Campaign (2021). Debt data portal. https://data.debtjustice.org. uk/ (retrieved 20/03/2023).

Katz, C. (2004). *Growing up Global: Economic Restructuring and Children's Everyday Lives*. Minneapolis: University of Minnesota Press.

LeBaron, G. (2016). Slavery, human trafficking, and forced labour: Implications for international development. In Grugel, J., Hammett, D. (eds) *The Palgrave Handbook of International Development* (pp. 381–398). London: Palgrave Macmillan.

Leftwich, A. (1995). Bringing politics back in: Towards a model of the developmental state. *The Journal of Development Studies*, 31 (3): 400–427.

McEwan, C. (2009). *Postcolonialism and Development*. Abingdon: Routledge.

Potter, R., Conway, D., Evans, R., Lloyd-Evans, S. (2012). *Key Concepts in Development Geography*. London: Sage.

Rasella, D., Aquino, R., Santos, C., Paes-Sousa, R., Barreto, M. (2013). Effect of a conditional cash transfer programme on childhood mortality: a nationwide analysis of Brazilian municipalities. *The Lancet*, 382 (9886): 57–64.

Rawlings, L., Rubio, G. (2005). Evaluating the impact of conditional cash transfer programs. *The World Bank Research Observer*, 20 (1): 29–55.

Rulli, M., Bellomi, D., Cazzoli, A., De Carolis, G., D'Odorico, P. (2016). The water-land-food nexus of first-generation biofuels. *Scientific Reports*, 6 (1): 1–10.

Schneider, F. (2016). Outside the state: The shadow economy and shadow economy labour force. In Grugel, J., Hammett, D. (eds) *The Palgrave Handbook of International Development* (pp. 185–203). London: Palgrave Macmillan.

Smith, J. (2010). *Biofuels and the Globalization of Risk: The Biggest Change in North-South Relationships since Colonialism?*London: Bloomsbury Publishing.

Sultana, F. (2020). Embodied intersectionalities of urban citizenship: Water, infrastructure, and gender in the Global South. *Annals of the American Association of Geographers*, 110 (5): 1407–1424.

UN (2019). 24 billion tons of fertile land lost every year, warns UN chief on World Day to Combat Desertification. Washington, DC: UN News. https://news.un.org/en/story/2019/06/1040561 (retrieved 20/03/2023).

UNCTAD (2022a). Global trade hits record high of $28.5 trillion in 2021, but likely to be subdued in 2022. Geneva: UNCTAD. https://unctad.org/news/global-trade-hits-record-high-285-trillion-2021-likely-be-subdued-2022 (retrieved 09/12/2022).

UNCTAD (2022b). *Trade and Development Report 2022. Development Prospects in a Fractured World: Global Disorder and Regional Responses*. Geneva: UNCTAD.

World Bank (1981). *Accelerated Development in Sub-Saharan Africa: An Agenda to Action*. Washington, DC: World Bank.

World Bank (2010). *World Development Report 2010: Development and Climate Change*. Washington, DC: World Bank.

World Bank (2022). Regional trade agreements. Washington, DC: World Bank. https://www.worldbank.org/en/topic/regional-integration/brief/regional-trade-agreements (retrieved 09/12/2022).

WTO (2022). *World Trade Statistical Review 2022*. Geneva: World Trade Organization. https://www.wto.org/english/res_e/publications_e/wtsr_2022_e.htm (retrieved 09/12/2022).

Wylde, C. (2016). The developmental state. In Grugel, J., Hammett, D. (eds) *The Palgrave Handbook of International Development* (pp. 121–138). London: Palgrave Macmillan.

WHY WE THINK DEVELOPMENT ONLY HAPPENS 'OVER THERE'

Global development always seems to happen somewhere else – at least for those of us in the global north. When government officials talk of development budgets and funding, these are aligned to the 'development needs' of overseas countries. At times when budgets are being cut, or popular media seeks to criticise development aid, this spending is positioned as in tension with the needs and priorities of both taxpayers and those 'in need' at home.

Here is a key issue: if global development truly is global (as the SDGs seek to remind us), then why do we not think of development challenges 'at home'? For those of us in the UK, Canada, or Finland 'global development' is something which (needs to) happen to others – or so it is commonly thought. Why is this? Ultimately it comes back to both the histories and power relations which inform development agendas *and* the everyday ways in which we are asked to think and talk about development. It seems Western politicians, media, and citizens have an aversion to publicly acknowledging that their countries also have development targets to meet.

We can see this clearly in Britain's House of Commons Library *Poverty in the UK* report from October 2021 (Francis-Devine, 2021) – nowhere in the 67-page report are the SDGs mentioned. This despite data showing that 11.7 million people (18% of the country's population) were living on relatively low income (rising to 14.5 million or 22% once housing costs were factored in) in 2019/2020 – a percentage almost unchanged for 12 years. Meanwhile, levels of children living in conditions of relatively low income have slowly increased (to 23% and 31% respectively). To

DOI: 10.4324/9781003155652-5

put this into context, for the UK to meet its SDG indicator 1.2 (to halve the proportion living in poverty according to national definitions) the country would need to reduce those living in relative poverty from 16.6% (2015) to 8.3% by 2030. The data on this do not look promising (you can find UK data for the SDGs here: http s://sdgdata.gov.uk/). While only one report, the failure to acknowledge the relevant SDG indicator can be seen as indicative of a broader tendency in both political and public thinking to assume that the *global* of global development only applies to the global south.

Remember the discussion earlier in the book about the language used to talk about development? The use of the terms First, Second, and Third Worlds, of 'developed' and 'developing' worlds, of global north and global south – these all ask us to think of development not only in spatial terms, but as separate or distant. The language used is laden with values and meanings which ultimately reinforce a dichotomy of the split between 'us' and 'them', those who are developed, and those needing development (Kothari, 2006). These narratives continue to play into the ways in which 'a nation imagines itself and constructs its identity through the reassertion of the home-nation as "developed" and "others" as "un/under-developed"' (Biccum, 2011: 1336). These processes reflect both historical and contemporary power relations, producing two groups – those like 'us' and those different to 'us' – through practices and processes of othering (Said, 1978; also see Jazeel, 2012). As a result, countries in the global north continue to position themselves as aspirational and superior – not only as the model to be followed but also offering self-justification for Western governments and development institutions to intervene in and impose development 'solutions' on other countries.

These narratives not only assume that 'development' or being 'developed' in particular ways (namely the material culture and economic condition of countries in the global north) is the aspired-to end point, but also assume Western or European ideas and experiences are the most valid or important. This idea is commonly known as Eurocentrism and assumes both the dominance or superiority of the West (in terms of knowledge, power, etc.) and that the 'north' is homogeneous. The result is that many dominant ideas, narratives about, and representations of development are rooted in Eurocentric ideas of modernity which typically reflect and embody the ideas of white, middle-class men from the global north (Willis, 2021).

PLACING DEVELOPMENT

So, how do these practices work on an everyday level? Let's start with thinking about how we view the world – in a literal sense. When you pick up a world map, what do you see? Land masses, oceans, political borders. These depictions – of national borders, of the names of countries, seas, and oceans – are powerful reminders of how language, power, and knowledge are integrated into development thinking and representations.

In some regions, particularly the African continent, many borders are reminders of colonial power and the ways in which European colonial powers arbitrarily created and imposed dividing lines between states. The names used for different countries and seas or oceans also reflect particular (geo-)political histories and power and challenges to these histories in the renaming of various states (for instance, the renaming of the Kingdom of Swaziland to the Kingdom of Eswatini in 2018 to mark 50 years of independence).

What about the layout and projection of the world map? Which region(s) or country/ies are central to the projection? Typically maps in the UK position the Greenwich Meridian line in the centre of the map, meaning the UK is prominently positioned. What happens, though, if we position the world map from a different perspective? Which countries/regions then appear at the core or centre of the map? This may sound like a minor and irrelevant consideration, but the continual, everyday messaging which locates particular places at the centre or periphery of a map is powerful: repeated exposure to such images leaves a political message not only of where 'we' are and where the global 'core' is, but also of where 'distant others' and the 'periphery' are.

In other words, Eurocentrism is given visual expression through Mercator projection maps, which locate Europe at the centre of the map. The Mercator projection then depicts continents and countries as they appear on a globe – but in 'unpeeling' the globe and moving from a three-dimensional to a two-dimensional representation, significant distortions appear. Specifically, those continents and countries further away from the equator are stretched and expanded – meaning those continents and countries closer to the equator appear disproportionately smaller.

While the Mercator projection remains commonplace, a contrasting projection called the Peters projection offers an alternative view of the world. Based on an equal area projection, this projection depicts countries and continents based on comparative land areas. While this means continents and countries may look distorted or stretched on a north–south axis, these maps give a far more realistic sense of the size and scale of equatorial land masses (while also displacing Europe from the centre of the map). However, the dominant representation of the world remains the Mercator projection – resultantly placing (an oversized) Europe at the heart of the picture.

DEVELOPMENT, REPRESENTATION, AND POPULAR CULTURE

Representations of 'other' people and places as inferior and in need of 'saving' and 'development' have a long history in popular culture. Cartoons and other media have long portrayed distant 'others' in negative and threatening ways, contrasting these with the supposed superiority of the Empire. Looking back to George Cruikshank's 1819 cartoon 'Blessing of the emigration to the Cape', we see the ways in which racism and 'othering' are used to depict European settlers being savaged by the indigenous population (Mason, 2010). With lions, crocodiles, and snakes as well as the (half-naked) indigenous population depicted as devouring settlers and their children, the reader is invited to view the Cape of Good Hope (in South Africa) and its inhabitants as exotic, primitive, beastly, and cannibalistic – a message reinforced in the caption: 'All among the Hottentots capering ashore; or the blessings of emigration to the Cape of Forlorn (Good) Hope (i.e.) to be half roasted by the sun and devoured by the natives'.

Similar depictions of the people, places, landscapes, and wildlife of countries in the global south proliferated during the colonial period, reiterating a Eurocentric message of superiority and justifying the 'civilising mission' of Empire. These practices are often talked about as 'othering' and an expression of 'orientalism'. These ideas, outlined by Edward Said (1978), argue that Western representations of the East (Asia, North Africa, and the Middle East) relied upon and promoted a set of negative, simplistic, and stereotypical ideas and images. In so doing, Said (1978) argued notions of Western superiority and Eurocentrism were reinforced through the exaggerating of differences between the 'us' of the West and the 'others' of the East, leading to prejudice and discrimination against those seen as different or from distant shores.

Through this process of 'othering', Said argues, images and imaginaries of the East as being irrational, backward, inferior, and in need of development, civilising, and saving are promoted. While originally written about Western depictions of the East, Said's argument has been widely used to critically discuss Western representations of 'others' across the globe: be this in relation to Joseph Conrad's classic 1899 novella *The Heart of Darkness* or contemporary media coverage of the global south in British newspapers.

Written at a time of extensive colonial exploration and exploitation of the African continent, during which the British explorer Henry Morton Stanley wrote of travelling *Through the Dark Continent* and *In Darkest Africa, The Heart of Darkness* tells the story of a fictional steamboat captain's journey along an unnamed African river and the descent into madness of Mr Kurtz, an ivory trader. Some have applauded the work for critiquing European colonialism in Africa and questioning the supposed superiority of colonialists. Others – including Chinua Achebe – have argued that the work dehumanised Africans, perpetuated racism, and a negative view of the African continent as savage and dangerous. The legacies of this novella are important in terms of representational practices, having been adapted into the 1979 film *Apocalypse Now* and inspiring the landscapes and storylines of the popular video games *Far Cry 2* and *Spec Ops: The Line*.

Returning to the nineteenth century briefly, we see how the idea of Africa as the 'dark' continent was mobilised to give an impression of a savage, barbaric, and dangerous place in need of the civilising mission of imperialism. Promoting the Empire-building project, these representations romanticised the vision of the white (male) saviour while contrasting the 'darkness' of Africa with the Enlightenment of the West. At the same time, these narratives positioned Africa as not only dangerous, but also exotic and alluring – a space for adventure and conquest, with particular gendered dynamics: for instance, African men were depicted as dangerous predators, white women as innocent and vulnerable.

DEVELOPMENT AND THE MEDIA

These stereotypes and practices of 'othering' are – unfortunately – still readily apparent in British (and, more broadly, Western) media coverage of events, people, and places of the global south. In much media coverage, as well as fundraising materials, we continue to see heavily raced and gendered images promoted. Stereotypes abound of (African) men as violent, brutal fighters or as criminals and a threat to social stability and safety – as in British newspaper coverage of the FIFA 2010 Football World Cup in South Africa (Hammett, 2011). Meanwhile, women are fetishised either as alluring and exotic or as vulnerable, agency-less visions of motherhood and womanhood in need of 'saving' (Dogra, 2011). Such concerns have contributed to Scott (2014) asking, 'What role can media play in addressing (or exacerbating) poverty and inequality?' While Scott offers a balanced argument about the potential for media in development, Sparks (2007: 7) provides a more positive or optimistic focus on 'the role that the media and other forms of communication can play in improving the conditions of life for the world's poorest people'.

Scott considers the use of different forms of media – from social media as a mobilisation tool, to the training of journalists in fragile countries, to fundraising adverts, and to foreign news coverage. There are, Scott (2014) argues, three main ways to think about media and development:

• *Communication for development* which is about dialogue to seek and realise sustained and meaningful change. This may be through the use of media for development in efforts to change norms and behaviours, or in a more participatory use of media in realising development outcomes. However, challenges in linking outcomes or change to media content can limit donor engagement with these strategies – despite the efforts of various organisations to argue that media can provide the 'magic bullet' for global development.

- *Media development* which is focused on supporting and strengthening the media sector within a country to support good governance and development outcomes.
- *Media representations of development* which examines the content and consequences of media representations of global development issues and countries in the global south (the main focus of the content that follows).

Implicit within these three approaches are considerations of the scales at which media are being produced and consumed (from grassroots to global media houses), the media platforms being used (from hand-printed or photocopied documents, through mass print and broadcast media, to the spaces of the internet and social media), and whether content is top-down, bottom-up, and supportive of or challenging dominant power (Sparks, 2007). Examples abound of the use of media-as-propaganda to support particular political and development ideologies and agendas – particularly pronounced during the Cold War – and techno-optimists continue to advocate for the potential of the internet to be a space of liberation and development.

While there is huge potential to explore the role of media and communication in or for development, our concern here is with media representations of development and how these not only place where development needs to happen in particular ways, but also establish to whom development needs to happen, by whom development is/can be done, and how development should be done and with what priorities. Before discussing the content of such coverage, it is important to reflect on how much coverage there is – how many news stories you see – relating to countries in the global south. In general, there is very limited coverage of issues, events, and news from the global south by media outlets in the West. This absence itself is important to note – highlighting how ideas of who, or where, counts are reflected in what/who/where is deemed worthy of coverage in the news.

If you think back over recent news stories about countries in the global south that you've seen, what have they focused on? How have they been framed? What language is used? What photos and other images are used? Repeated analysis of British or Western media coverage of countries in the global south highlights the continued practices of 'othering' and use of lazy stereotypes and generalisations which speak to a distancing between – and constructed superiority/inferiority of – the global north and global south. In particular, Western media coverage is often framed in negative ways (about crises, disasters, poverty); emphasises and sensationalises questions of crime, violence, and safety; and mobilises a binary or dichotomy between 'us' (the Western readers) and 'them' (the citizens of the global south) that reinforces ideas of the 'dangerous other' and the 'vulnerable us' (Hammett, 2014; Mishra, 2012; Schallhorn, 2019).

REPRESENTATION AND DEVELOPMENT FUNDRAISING

Alternatively, we can consider the adverts you see during commercial breaks on television or that pop up on your social media feed. Think of those that you may have seen from organisations such as Water Aid, Oxfam, the British Red Cross, or the Disasters Emergency Committee. What images do they show? What words are used in the voice-overs? And whose voices are used?

These representational practices can be understood as part of broader media practices which classically 'reduce Africa [and other regions in the global south] to a series of stereotypes of chaos and disaster' (Mercer et al., 2003: 422). These narrative practices – witnessed around environmental hazards, conflicts, and sporting mega-events – continually position countries in the global south as 'other', as dangerous and threatening, and, ultimately, as in need of 'civilising' and development (Hammett, 2014, 2019).

Within the global development sector, tendencies to present simplistic and sensationalist representations of the impoverished, needy other are worryingly common. Such tendencies are not new. The video and other promotional materials surrounding the 1984 Band Aid charity single 'Do They Know It's Christmas' not only stripped away the agency of the Ethiopian people in responding to the famine but depoliticised the crisis by failing to acknowledge the role of the West (and Russia) in fuelling the proxy war that destabilised the region and contributed significantly to the famine. With the representational practices focused solely upon environmental causes for the 1983–1985 Ethiopian famine, these overlooked and marginalised the national and global political factors which contributed to the lack of food security in the region (Müller, 2013). More than this, as a defining moment in celebrity humanitarianism, the imagery of poverty, starvation, and despair established a common frame and language for use in subsequent humanitarian appeals. As a result, popular representations in development charity campaigns often speak to a specific vision of an 'imagined Africa' which is mired in poverty, disease, starvation, and violence. These practices ask us to feel pity rather than demand justice (Müller, 2013: 470), and from this to act as saviours for the helpless and needy. In other words, such depictions ask us – as the viewer or spectator – to make the decision to intervene, emphasising our agency and power and reinforcing a paternalistic, white saviour approach. At the same time, these depictions strip away the power and agency of those represented. This process means not only that the imagined difference and distance between 'us' and 'them' are reinforced, but also that the global order is retained.

The legacies of Band Aid live on, not only in the release of new versions of the song in 1989, 2004, and 2014, but also in the repeated deployment of stereotypical representations of distant others. These practices continue to reinscribe particular perceptions, assumptions, and stereotypes which both dehumanise and disempower those depicted. As we will explore, when thinking about how global development is represented, it is crucial to ask how places and peoples are represented as 'needing' or 'deserving' development, and who can deliver this development?

Pause for a moment, and imagine you've turned on the TV and hit the advert break, or you've cued up your next video on YouTube and the pre-video adverts are playing. You are presented with a montage of images of a sad-looking girl walking over a patch of bare ground with a plastic bottle to take water from a river, with cows drinking on the other side. Moments later, a famous actor provides a narration over another montage of images, this time of tarpaulin tents flapping in the wind under a sunny sky and then a woman and child sitting in a medical tent – the voice-over telling you of their plight and how a donation from you could provide much-needed medicine or food.

Sound familiar? Probably. These are the typical styles in which global development charities have, for many years, sought to pull on the viewers' heartstrings and – most importantly – to open their purses and wallets. Pause for a moment – how did the people in the adverts look in your mind? Whom did the voice-over actor sound like? What did the background landscape look like? It probably wasn't imagery of a tired, white middle-class hillwalker collecting water in the highlands of Scotland, nor was it likely to have been of a family in England waiting for their Covid-19 vaccination or queuing for a food bank.

Why does this matter? It matters because it illustrates not only that charity advertising is driven, in part, by dictates of the market and audience responsiveness but also how the continued use of paternalist and stereotypical narratives produces imagined geographies of global development – that it happens 'over there'. Charity advertising has continually represented an imagined homogenised, poverty-stricken other needing pity and care. This 'victim frame' positions (potential) aid and development recipients as lacking agency and power, as passively awaiting benevolent support and upliftment (Hammett, 2019; Vossen et al., 2018).

Not convinced? OK, what about Ed Sheeran's 2017 Red Nose Day appeal? In this short video, Sheeran is shown meeting with street children in Liberia's capital Freetown: but rather than giving voice and agency to these young people, their dignity is stripped away and we hear of Sheeran's feelings of guilt and shame. The language and imagery are used to convey a sense of desperation, of fear, of dependency that you, the viewer, have the agency to overcome simply by donating £5 or £10. The Ed Sheeran video, as with BBC journalist Stacey Dooley's posting on social media photos of her holding a Ugandan boy during filming for 2019 Comic Relief, conveyed a 'white saviour' message which perpetuates a Eurocentric view of global development.

This positioning of (typically) white, Western celebrities as the face of global development interventions, and the narrative that the (typically) white viewer at home can then 'save' Africa, remain common. The 'white gaze' seen in these fundraising commercials views and locates people and societies through a lens which assumes white superiority and reinforces understandings and measurements of development in relation to Eurocentric experiences (Peace Direct, 2021). In this process, the agency of those depicted is removed: the European viewer is instead presented as the person with the power and agency to make change – to resolve the development challenge being depicted. This strips away not only the agency, but also the voice and dignity of those being depicted as in need of development. It is assumed that the Western viewer knows best as to what is needed, how development should be defined, prioritised, and measured.

These disempowering and Eurocentric narratives inform a broader set of problematic and simplistic representational practices which have long been used in the global development industry to support fundraising efforts. These practices focus on charity rather than (social) justice, removing power and agency from while also silencing those depicted as (potential) recipients and perpetuating negative and degrading narratives of corruption, poverty, inferiority, and victimhood (Cameron, 2015; Schwartz and Richey, 2019). In short, they continually reinforce an imagined geography of development: a geography in which development happens to 'others' who are 'over there'.

SATIRICAL RESPONSES TO STEREOTYPICAL REPRESENTATIONS

In light of the prevalence of such practices in development fundraising adverts, the Norwegian Students and Academics' International Fund (SAIH) established the 'Radi-Aid' awards. These awards, which ran from 2013 to 2017, celebrated the best and worst of global development charity fundraising films. Each year the worst examples of victim framing, stereotyping, and – at times – racist depictions in fundraising adverts were awarded the 'Rusty Radiator', while the film which placed greatest emphasis upon agency and voices of recipients and/or which best debunked stereotypical ideas received the 'Golden Radiator'.

Why the Radi-Aid awards, you might be asking? The campaign started with SAIH making satirical videos that challenged dominant representations in development fundraising videos. Their 2012 'Africa for Norway' video offered a satirical challenge to the video for the Live Aid 'Do They Know It's Christmas' charity single. Inverting the gaze and narrative, the Africa for Norway video featured a series of African musicians and celebrities coming together to raise money for – and collect – oil-filled radiators to provide warmth for those living in the cold of a Scandinavian winter. Not only did the video highlight how Western development sector depictions of 'Africa' impose a homogeneous imagery upon the continent, but also (through the request to send oil-filled radiators to Norway) it critiqued how Western development initiatives impose 'solutions' from a distance without understanding the local context and ignore the broader (geo-)political and economic structures which frame global poverty, debt, and inequality (Cameron, 2015; Fridell, 2013; Schwartz and Richey, 2019). Other satirical videos from SAIH have focused on the damage caused by simplistic, stereotypical representations of Africa and the shortcomings of the international volunteer industry and 'white saviourism'.

Building on these interventions, the Radi-Aid awards were launched in response to the 'need to change the way fund raising campaigns are communicating issues of poverty and development' (SAIH, 2013). Amongst the winners of and nominees for the Rusty Radiator Awards were videos from Save the Children USA, Feed a Child South Africa, Band Aid 20, Humanitarian Aid Foundation, and Comic Relief. Jury comments on these videos noted how they stripped away dignity, were patronising, amounted to 'poverty porn' and 'poverty tourism', promoted a white saviour complex, amounted to bullying, stripped away agency and power, and, on occasion, were outright racist – with the 2014 Rusty winner 'using the same stereotypes to both raise awareness and steal agency. The poor are already depicted as incapable of their own rescue, now they are being compared to dogs' (SAIH, 2014a). The 2015 Rusty Radiator winner, Band Aid 30, was condemned for continuing the 'spread of misinformation and stereotypes of Africa as a country filled with misery and diseases … Highly offensive and awful in every way possible' (SAIH, 2015). The 2016 nominee from Save the Children Netherlands was castigated as:

> the epitome of 'poverty pornography' as it focuses solely on the bare lives of the suffering children and fetishizes their bodies (e.g. their swollen bellies because of starvation). It presents people in the South as helpless and unable to overcome their sufferings without help from the outside.
>
> (SAIH, 2016)

While the 2016 winner from Compassion International:

promote[d] deep-rooted perceptions of Western superiority over the South. It reinforces the white savior complex, and depicts that there is nothing the parents can do for their children other than to wait for the sponsor who can save their lives and their future.

(SAIH, 2016)

Golden Radiator nominees and winners included SOS Children's Villages Norway, Save the Children UK, Kinderpostzegels, WaterAid, White Helmets in Syria, Plan International UK, War Child Holland, and Ba Futuru/Oaktree. Feedback emphasised how these videos 'emphasise[d] the universality of suffering and empathy, and br[oke] racial stereotypes about who suffers' (SAIH, 2014b), 'skew[ed] away from the typical depiction of poverty' (SAIH, 2017), revealed disparities between idealised and real worlds, educated viewers and empowered individuals, and spoke to development concerns in both the global north and global south in creative and empathetic ways (see also Schwartz and Richey, 2019).

Set against the backdrop of the Syrian war, the War Child Holland video powerfully conveys the pressing humanitarian challenges of the conflict without stripping agency or dehumanising the parent or the child. The Ba Futuro/Oaktree video, 'I must not make assumptions', offers a satirical commentary of typical global development imagery and assumptions. Through a clever juxtaposition of footage and (increasingly confused) commentary from the voice-over artist the video dismantles assumptions about levels of development, rural and urban landscapes, access to education, and other classic narratives of development.

What these videos – and other Rusty and Golden Radiator nominees and winners – demonstrate is the power and influence of media and representation on how we think of development, where we assume it must happen, and to whom. Content which perpetuates the 'othering' and 'over there-ing' of development is often known as poverty porn – mobilising white saviour narratives and stripping away the agency of those depicted as in 'need' of our support. As Fridell (2013) notes, these types of fundraising narrative from global development NGOs end up reinforcing rather than challenging the (global) power relations and structural inequalities that are integral to the development landscape. Instead, they become 'implementing agencies for donor-driven aid and aid policy' (Fridell, 2013: 1493).

Radi-Aid is not the only initiative to try to tackle 'othering' and other problematic representational practices in relation to global development and humanitarianism. Social media-based campaigns including Barbie Saviour (Instagram) and Humanitarians of Tinder (Tumblr) have also used humour to rebuke stereotypical representational practices and call out Eurocentrism (Schwartz and Richey, 2019). These parodies challenge not only the ways in which NGOs represent their work, but also how travellers, volunteers, and others also reiterate and perpetuate imageries of development and othering.

While Rusty Radiator-esque representations continue, there are some signs of change in the ways in which global development is depicted in daily life. Following the widespread outcry over the tone and focus of their videos and under pressure over the colonial and victim gaze within them, Red Nose Day committed to changing their approach to fundraising for 2021 and onwards. Rather than using footage of malnourished children and sending Western celebrities overseas to front the recorded materials, Red Nose Day changed direction to focus on hiring local filmmakers to tell stories from local communities and giving agency to local voices.

DEPOLITICISING GLOBAL DEVELOPMENT

Crucially, even with these signs of change and the rise in parodies and critiques of 'othering' and 'over there-ing', the ways in which global development is talked about continue to depoliticise the issue. Depoliticise may seem an odd term to use initially – in the UK, the budget for global development (and our supposed commitment to spending 0.7% of GDP on global development) is in many ways highly politicised by politicians and the media. In recent years, we've witnessed outcries over the provision of global development aid to India at a time when the Indian government was funding a space programme, and the political rhetoric of the need to address domestic needs first given levels of poverty in the UK (interestingly these calls are never linked to the UK's SDG targets). So, yes, global development is inherently political, and global development budgets are often highly politicised.

What I mean by the 'depoliticisation' of global development within representational practices is that fundraising and other media coverage of development issues tend to ignore or remove the political structures which frame development 'needs'. More broadly, Rist (2007) argues that the ubiquitous use of the term 'development' to capture any and all policies and ideas which were seen as 'doing good' and improving poor people's lives has created a new vision of the world: one in which un/under/developed and development are naturalised as part of the world order, rather than being constructed from social and political actions and narratives. This is a process of depoliticisation – and one that is continually reinforced in various ways.

As references to the historic and contemporary political, social, and economic structures which underpin inequalities, poverty, and power relations are omitted, the critical questions regarding the how, why, and where of 'development' are silenced. Instead, the assumption becomes entrenched that the poor are poor because either they are unable or unwilling to help themselves, their governments are too corrupt to care, or their environment is too marginal or hostile to support life. The media coverage and subsequent Band Aid fundraising campaign in the 1980s (discussed earlier) in response to the famine in the Horn of Africa is a prime (albeit very dated) example of this.

CELEBRITY DEVELOPMENT

Band Aid can also be seen as one of the earliest high-profile cases of celebrity development (or perhaps development celebrities), triggering subsequent expansion in celebrities becoming involved in and promoting global development causes and initiatives. The roles of celebrities in global development vary widely: from fronting fundraising efforts and videos, to taking up advocacy or 'ambassador' roles for the United Nations or a major NGO, launching or backing 'causerism'-based consumption brands, educational and policy advocacy activities, or launching their own global development initiatives (such as Madonna's *Raising Malawi* project or Oprah Winfrey's Charitable Foundation or the *Not on*

Our Watch organisation backed by Don Cheadle, George Clooney, Matt Damon, and others). In some instances, a celebrity's role can be driven by genuine interest and concern. At other times, as critics have argued, their involvement may be driven out of self-interest (to be a celebrity, one needs a public profile and fronting a message about 'doing good' is an effective way of building this profile). At the same time, if the focus is on the celebrity (rather than the issue) the viewers' focus is turned back upon themselves – replicating the ideas of white saviourism. Other critiques have argued that these practices continue to depoliticise the structural causes of poverty or inequality, and may actually reinforce these through the promotion of consumption-based global development 'solutions' (Brockington, 2014a).

So, what are the potential costs and benefits for the tie-in between celebrities and global development agendas and institutions? Why might UNICEF, Oxfam, or any other organisation seek celebrity endorsement? For the global development agency or NGO, their hopes will be that having a celebrity onboard will gain their efforts (social) media coverage and audience engagement, lead to increased financial donations and other forms of support, provide legitimacy that their organisation is sufficiently important to be taken seriously, and that the celebrity will also ease access to senior figures and officials. For the celebrity, the benefits can include a positive public profile, the possibility to have access to powerful individuals, financial reward or payments for their endorsement, or the possibility to promote their own brands and products as part of causerism campaigns. This is not to discount the altruistic motives of many celebrities, who commit to supporting causes that they have an interest in and who recognise that they can leverage their status and standing for the benefit of others (Brockington, 2014b). These considerations frame the appointment of Angelina Jolie, Liam Neeson, Serena Williams, Jackie Chan, and many others as UNICEF ambassadors, Don Cheadle as a UN Environment Programme Goodwill Ambassador, and Harrison Ford's support for the Alliance of Rainforests.

However, as well as the aforementioned critiques we also see occasions where the links between celebrity and global development go wrong. Audiences may grow weary of celebrities who 'do development' and dominate narratives (for instance Bob Geldof, Bono); in other situations scandals around either the celebrity or development organisation can backfire and negatively affect the reputation of all parties involved. More widely, the media can play a vital role in relation to celebrity-backed or -founded global development initiatives through a process dubbed 'tabloid accountability' (Budabin et al., 2017). While these initiatives may be sustained through elite networks, without the need to rely upon public fundraising to operate, critical media coverage of scandals surrounding Oprah's South African schools and controversies with Madonna's *Raising Malawi* project remains important (Budabin et al., 2017).

REFERENCES

Biccum, A. (2011). Marketing development: Celebrity politics and the 'new' development advocacy. *Third World Quarterly*, 32 (7): 1331–1346.

Brockington, D. (2014a). The production and construction of celebrity advocacy in international development. *Third World Quarterly*, 35 (1): 88–108.

Brockington, D. (2014b). *Celebrity Advocacy and International Development*. Abingdon: Routledge.

Budabin, A.C., Rasmussen, L.M., Richey, L.A. (2017). Celebrity-led development organisations: The legitimating function of elite engagement. *Third World Quarterly*, 38 (9): 1952–1972.

Cameron, J.D. (2015). Can poverty be funny? The serious use of humour as a strategy of public engagement for global justice. *Third World Quarterly*, 36 (2): 274–290.

Dogra, N. (2011). The mixed metaphor of 'Third World woman': Gendered representations by international development NGOs. *Third World Quarterly*, 32 (2): 333–348.

Francis-Devine, B. (2021). *Poverty in the UK: Statistics*. London: House of Commons Library. https://researchbriefings.files.parliament.uk/documents/SN07096/SN07096.pdf (retrieved 24/10/2022).

Fridell, G. (2013). Introduction—politicising debt and development: Activist voices on social justice in the new millennium. *Third World Quarterly*, 34 (8): 1492–1496.

Hammett, D. (2011). British media representations of South Africa and the 2010 FIFA World Cup. *South African Geographical Journal*, 93 (1): 63–74.

Hammett, D. (2014). Tourism images and British media representations of South Africa. *Tourism Geographies*, 16 (2): 221–236.

Hammett, D. (2019). Whose development? Power and space in international development. *Geography*, 104 (1): 12–18.

Jazeel, T. (2012). Postcolonialism: Orientalism and the geographical imagination. *Geography*, 97 (1): 4–11.

Kothari, U. (2006). Critiquing "race" and racism in development discourse and practice. *Progress in Development Studies*, 6 (1): 1–7.

Mason, A. (2010). The cannibal ogre and the rape of justice: A contrapuntal reading. *Critical African Studies*, 2 (4): 32–64.

Mercer, C., Mohan, G., Power, M. (2003). Towards a critical political geography of African development. *Geoforum*, 34 (4): 419–436.

Mishra, S. (2012). 'The Shame Games': A textual analysis of Western press coverage of the Commonwealth Games in India. *Third World Quarterly*, 33 (5): 871–886.

Müller, T.R. (2013). The long shadow of Band Aid humanitarianism: Revisiting the dynamics between famine and celebrity. *Third World Quarterly*, 34 (3): 470–484.

Peace Direct (2021). *Time to Decolonise Aid: Insights and Lessons from a Global Consultation*. London: Peace Direct.

Rist, G. (2007). Development as a buzzword. *Development in Practice*, 17 (4/5): 485–491.

Said, E. (1978). *Orientalism*. London: Penguin.

SAIH (2013). The Rusty Radiator Awards 2013. Oslo: SAIH. https://www.radiaid.com/radiator-awards-2013/ (retrieved 14/07/2022).

SAIH (2014a). The Rusty Radiator Award 2014. Oslo: SAIH. https://www.radiaid.com/rusty-radiator-award-2014/ (retrieved 14/07/2022).

SAIH (2014b). The Golden Radiator Award 2014. Oslo: SAIH. https://www.radiaid.com/golden-radiator-award-2014/ (retrieved 14/07/2022).

SAIH (2015). The Rusty Radiator Award 2015. Oslo: SAIH. https://www.radiaid.com/rusty-radiator-award-2015 (retrieved 14/07/2022).

SAIH (2016). The Rusty Radiator Award 2016. Oslo: SAIH. https://www.radiaid.com/rusty-radiator-award-2016/ (retrieved 14/07/2022).

SAIH (2017). The Golden Radiator Award 2017. Oslo: SAIH. https://www.radiaid.com/radi-aid-awards-2017 (retrieved 14/07/2022).

Schallhorn, C. (2019). "The land of football": An analysis of media coverage of the 2014 FIFA World Cup and its effects on people's perceptions of Brazil. *International Journal of Intercultural Relations*, 72: 25–35.

Schwartz, K., Richey, L.A. (2019). Humanitarian humor, digilantism, and the dilemmas of representing volunteer tourism on social media. *New Media and Society*, 21 (9): 1928–1946.

Scott, M. (2014). *Media and Development*. London: Zed Books.

Sparks, C. (2007). *Globalization, Development and the Mass Media*. London: SAGE.

Vossen, M., Van Gorp, B., Schulpen, L. (2018). In search of the pitiful victim: A frame analysis of Dutch, Flemish and British newspapers and NGO-advertisements. *Journal of International Development*, 30 (4): 643–660.

Willis, K. (2021). *Theories and Practices of Development*. Abingdon: Routledge.

CONTESTING THE DEVELOPMENT LANDSCAPE

When we think of global development, the common presumption is that countries and organisations in the global north act as donors to recipients in the global south. As chapter 5 outlined, these perceptions are often based upon campaigns aimed at encouraging you to donate money to relieve suffering during a humanitarian crisis or to support other development projects. At the same time, we repeatedly hear about the 0.7% of GDP target for overseas development assistance (ODA) spending by governments. Agreed as a UN resolution in 1970, this non-binding target remains a stated goal of many countries – although only a few (Sweden, Denmark, Luxembourg, Norway, and the UK) have repeatedly met this over the intervening years.

The landscape is far more complex. Rivalries during the Cold War, legacies of empire, and continuing national self-interest mean the donor landscape in the global north is varied. There are longstanding traditions of development cooperation and support between countries in the global south, and we are seeing new donors – and new forms of donors – emerging. In short, the development funding landscape is evolving and shifting, with recent policy turns seeing 'traditional' donors increasingly emphasising the role of the private sector in promoting development with a growing focus on trade and investment, and a very clear re-linking of aid to national interests and broader foreign policy goals.

WHAT IS DEVELOPMENT AID?

Before we think about the different donors and strategies involved in development, it is useful to ask: What is development aid? And

DOI: 10.4324/9781003155652-6

is it good? A simple definition for development aid could be considered as being the provision of support for 'development among the poorest people in the world, among the most marginalized and oppressed people and societies' (Degnbol-Martinussen and Engberg-Pedersen, 2003: xv). As explored in this chapter, development aid comes in many forms and is provided through various institutions and processes. Broadly understood, aid encompasses any form of ODA, concessionary loan, grant or other support including technical support, structural adjustment policies, medical and military aid, and so on provided to promote development and welfare (Goldin, 2018). In simple terms, development aid may be provided by governments, NGOs, international organisations, development banks, and philanthropists in various forms – including money, debt relief, food relief, humanitarian support, training and expertise, food or other basic supplies, as well as resources and personnel in specific sectors (for instance education or health-care).

Within this broader landscape, what is commonly called *foreign aid* encompasses ODA, loans, and grants. ODA refers to the flow of funds and assistance (in the form of grants and soft loans) from governments and other official agencies to multilateral organisations and countries in the global south to promote economic development and welfare. Military aid and other security-related support are excluded from measures of ODA.

Flows of aid occur in various ways, amongst the most common of which is through the direct provision of support from one state to another. This is known as *bilateral aid*. Major providers of bilateral aid include the US, Germany, the UK, and Japan. Aid may also be delivered through major institutions such as the World Bank, with funding provided from multiple donors – this is known as *multilateral aid*. In addition to these major flows of development aid we see the provision of development aid via the NGO sector (for instance the Rockefeller Foundation, Oxfam), and via more recent *philanthropic foundations* (such as the Bill and Melinda Gates Foundation).

For some, development aid is an altruistic action which supports the well-being of others – drawing upon our goodwill, we offer help to others. This sense of altruism is key for public fundraising campaigns but also underpins popular public sentiment for Western governments to provide ODA funding. For others, aid can be a means of offering reparations for past injustices and exploitations, or a means of assuaging colonial guilt. For yet others, aid is seen as a tool of self-interest – another form of power through which the rich and powerful continue to dominate global politics and economy. Key concerns raised here often relate to the use of aid monies (or the threat of withholding aid) to drive political or social changes in recipient countries – and while this may be done to promote human rights or force anti-corruption initiatives, it can also be a tool of ideology, to 'turn' or maintain a political bent in leadership. In other instances, aid is used as a tool of diplomacy with expectations for future support in votes at the UN or in other diplomatic spaces.

The provision – or withholding – of development aid is a key tool of statecraft and power, often reflecting political rather than economic needs, or (when withheld) used as a sanction to seek to effect change in the recipient state. In broader terms these are understood as 'conditionalities' – aid is provided in return for the recipient state doing something that the donor has requested. For some, these dynamics are simply the continued exercise of power by the powerful; for others they are an essential but insufficient mechanism for tackling key issues or challenges. The use of these by the World Bank and IMF in relation to Poverty Reduction Strategy Papers and the imposing of neoliberal economic orthodoxy has been a major focus of criticism particularly since the 2005 Paris Declaration.

The rapid emergence of China (amongst other states) as a key provider of development finance in recent decades has been linked to the lack of conditionalities they impose upon recipients relating to expectations or commitments to democracy, human rights, or good governance. While many have been strongly critical of China's willingness to provide development loans and funding to countries with poor human rights records or authoritarian leaders, supporters argue that this approach is more equitable and free of the power relations and colonial histories that are linked to many 'traditional' donors.

Aid may also be provided with myriad caveats and conditionalities which require domestic economic restructuring or changes to government spending, or which require the recipient state to then spend some or all of the aid on services, materials, or expertise bought from the donor country. These latter practices are known as 'tied aid' or 'boomerang aid'. While supporters argue that this form of aid limits the potential for corruption and theft by recipients, critics note the continued risk of corruption from the donor side and that tied aid often serves the economic interests of donors rather than effectively supporting development outcomes for recipients. For some donors the use of tied aid is a deliberate economic and geopolitical strategy: Ganga and Girod (2019) report that in the early 2000s USAID openly admitted that tied overseas development aid primarily benefited US companies and employment, and that tied aid was used as a predatory strategy to 'capture' emerging markets. For recipients, Ganga and Girod (2019) argue, tied aid actually *decelerates* economic growth and development by discouraging domestic investment and productivity, and can often end up consolidating the wealth and power of elites while offering limited benefits to the poor. These concerns were highlighted by scandals during the 1990s and early 2000s surrounding tied aid from the UK to Malaysia (for the Pergau Dam) and Tanzania (for a radar system), which involved massive overcharging by British suppliers.

WHO ARE THE MAIN DONORS AND RECIPIENTS?

ODA from the OECD Development Assistance Committee (DAC) has increased from $37.6 billion in 1960 to $162.2 billion in 2020. While the growth in ODA was slow during the 1960s (rising to $42.2 billion in 1970), rapid increases followed in the 1970s (to $62.2 billion in 1980) and 1980s (to $82 billion in 1990) before dropping during the 1990s (to $76.83 billion in 2000) and then rapidly increasing after the turn of the millennium (to $129.1 billion in 2020). While the dollar amount has increased, the percentage of DAC members' GDP spent on ODA has not – indeed it has dropped from a high of 0.54% in 1964, bottoming-out at a low of 0.21% in 2001 before rising to 0.33% in 2020. In 2021 official ODA reached $178.9 billion, including over $6 billion for Covid vaccines, $18.8 billion on humanitarian aid, $9.3 billion on supporting refugees within donor states, and just $545 million on debt relief (OECD, 2022). While this may be the highest amount ever provided in ODA, it remained far below the UN's 0.7% target.

In 2020, official ODA flows to regions around the world ranged from $1.9 billion to Oceania, to $2.8 billion to Europe, $7.7

billion to America, $29.7 billion to Asia, $33.8 billion to Africa, as well as $38.9 billion on other 'unspecified' support for developing country recipients (Table 6.1). The top ten recipients of ODA (in absolute rather than per capita terms) were Bangladesh ($3.2 billion), Syria ($2.4 billion), Afghanistan ($2.3 billion), Ethiopia ($2.3 billion), Jordan ($2.2 billion), India ($2.1 billion), Iraq ($2.0 billion), Somalia ($2.0 billion), Myanmar ($1.9 billion), and Colombia ($1.7 billion) (OECD.Stat, 2022).

The largest DAC ODA donors in 2021 were the US ($42.3 billion), Germany ($32.2 billion), Japan ($17.6 billion), UK ($15.8 billion), and France ($15.4 billion), while the smallest were the Czech Republic ($362 million), Greece ($264 million), Slovak Republic ($151 million), Slovenia ($115 million), and Iceland ($72

Table 6.1 Regional and sub-regional disbursements of official ODA, 2020

Recipient	Amount
Europe	$2.8 billion
Africa	$33.8 billion
–North Africa	$2.2 billion
–Sub-Saharan Africa	$29.3 billion
–Regional	$2.3 billion
America	$7.7 billion
–Caribbean and Central America	$3.1 billion
–South America	$3.9 billion
–Regional	$675 million
Asia	$29.7 billion
–Far East Asia	$4.8 billion
–South and Central Asia	$13.2 billion
–Middle East	$10.7 billion
–Regional	$1.1 billion
Oceania	$1.9 billion
–Melanesia	$871 million
–Micronesia	$366 million
–Polynesia	$274 million
'Unspecified'	$38.9 billion

Source: Data from OECD.Stat (2022)

million). However, as a percentage of Gross National Income (GNI), the top DAC donors were Luxembourg (0.99%; $539 million), Norway (0.93%; $4.7 billion), Sweden (0.92%; $5.9billion), Germany (0.74%), and Denmark (0.7%; $2.9 billion). Of the other top five spenders, France provided 0.52% of GNI as ODA, the UK 0.5%, Japan 0.34%, and the US 0.18% – placing it joint 23rd (with Portugal) out of the 29 DAC donor countries according to percentage of GDP (ahead of only South Korea, Poland, Czech Republic, Slovak Republic, and Greece) (Donortracker, 2022).

IS DEVELOPMENT AID A GOOD THING?

One of the most powerful anti-aid advocates, the neoliberal economist Dambisa Moyo (2009: xix) argues that 'Aid has been and continues to be, an unmitigated political, economic and humanitarian disaster', and that despite more than $1 trillion of aid being transferred to Africa, the continent is worse off as a result. Moyo's stance contrasts significantly with those like Degnbol-Martinussen and Engberg-Pedersen (2003: xv) who argue that 'no other, better way exists that can replace foreign aid as part of a solidary effort to achieve greater equality between countries … and between people within developing countries.'

Amongst Moyo's concerns, she argues that an overreliance on development aid has led to aid dependency, corruption, and the entrenching of poverty. This, she claims, results in a never-ending cycle in which aid recipients continually require further aid transfers. Echoing these concerns, Cosgrove and Curtis (2018: 39) argue that if overseas development aid accounts for over 60% of a recipient state's budget this has a profoundly negative effect on economic growth and development, causes prices to rise, contributes to corruption, and supports autocratic governance.

More broadly, concerns remain that overseas development aid remains largely driven by donor self-interest, particularly in relation to national security concerns and economic opportunities. As a result, development aid can be seen as reinforcing power inequalities (particularly so when colonial histories frame donor–recipient relations) and maintaining the global political status quo – particularly when access to development funding is contingent upon conditionalities imposed by politically and economically powerful donors and institutions. In recent years there has also been growing disquiet over the manipulation of rules on the use of development aid to allow the increasing use of these funds to support the costs of supporting and processing refugees and asylum seekers within donor states.

Meanwhile, advocates for development aid argue that these financial (and other) flows are vital to efforts to realise the SDGs, reduce poverty, tackle diseases, and improve the quality of life of millions around the world. The belief is that development aid will promote economic growth in the recipient state, with this growth then driving a self-reinforcing multiplier effect (i.e. that economic growth creates more jobs and leads to more money circulating in the local economy, leading to increased tax revenues which are then re-invested in economic growth and welfare provisions, and so the cycle repeats). Critics meanwhile point out that the benefits of economic growth are too often either retained by a small (political or economic) elite or extracted from the local by major corporations.

Others contend that overseas development aid remains important but implementation may be ineffective due to poor management by donors and/or recipients or because interventions are badly aligned to local needs or have ineffective targets and approaches. For instance, it is widely recognised that improving schooling outcomes, particularly for girls, is hugely beneficial for development outcomes. But what specific intervention(s) would contribute most effectively to realising this goal? Would it be providing more textbooks? Offering free school meals? Having more (and better-trained) teachers? Extending the school day?

These questions have challenged development policy makers for years – and in 2019 Abhijit Banerjee, Esther Duflo, and Michael Kremer were awarded the Nobel Prize for Economics for their work in developing experimental approaches to such dilemmas (Banerjee and Duflo, 2011). (Their answer to the question of how to best improve schooling outcomes related to the way that teaching was delivered.)

Whichever side of these debates you find yourself on, development aid remains an integral component of the global development landscape: between 1970 and 2005 ODA to Africa was greater than other financial flows (Serieux, 2018: 327). It is also one that is being given new impetus with growing demands for – and first steps by the EU and select other countries towards providing – 'loss and damage' compensation to poorer nations to rebuild and recover from extreme weather events and climate-related disasters. With the costs incurred from the impacts of extreme weather events running into the hundreds of billions of dollars a year, both bi- and multi-lateral aid packages responding to these disasters will increasingly come to the fore of development aid agendas.

TYPES OF AID

Aid can mean very different things – it may be provided as financial support, technical advice, political support, or preferential trade agreements, and can often involve a degree of reciprocity, two-way flow. As critics point out, the required or expected payback (be this financial, political, or other) often serves to reinforce dominant power relations, and asserts power over the recipients.

Aid can also be focused upon different needs and priorities. The most common forms include:

- *Humanitarian aid/relief*, which is commonly a short-term venture to meet immediate need through the provision of food, water, medicine, shelter, and other essentials to those affected by environmental disasters or human conflicts. These interventions are – under the Geneva Convention of 1949 – required to be impartial, neutral, and independent, meaning they are guided by needs and accessible to all in need, that development agencies do not take sides and act independently of state control. However, the growing role of the military in either delivering or providing security to allow the delivery of humanitarian aid is creating challenges to this principle (O'Keefe and Rose, 2014).
- *Development aid*, which is typically part of a longer-term vision to promote economic, social, and/or political development within a country. Support may be provided through technical expertise and advice or financially in the form of grants, loans, or investment in infrastructure or other major projects.

Humanitarian aid is dominated by donor governments, the UN (primarily through UNICEF, UNHCR, WFP, FAO, and OCHA), the International Red Cross and Red Crescent Movement (ICRC), and INGOs (O'Keefe and Rose, 2014). The need for humanitarian aid is growing due to increasing numbers and severity of environmental disasters – at the time of writing, Pakistan has experienced massive flooding and warnings abound of drought and impending famine in the Horn of Africa – as well as environmental- and conflict-induced displacement leading to growing numbers of refugees and internally displaced peoples (IDPs).

Critics have argued that the division between humanitarian/ emergency relief and development aid is problematic – that recovery from a disaster cannot be delivered solely through the short-term meeting of basic needs. This has led to the emergence of a 'humanitarian aid plus' approach amongst some donors who combine emergency relief with support for rehabilitation and development funding to support sustainable recovery and, where relevant, conflict prevention (O'Keefe and Rose, 2014). .

More widely, common weaknesses in humanitarian aid provision include limited coordination and oversight of development activities meaning multiple organisations may try to deliver the same support leading to duplication of efforts and waste of resources – while other needs may not be delivered. Similarly, popular mobilisations to support immediate need – as witnessed in the response to Russia's invasion of Ukraine, when individuals and small groups rushed to provide blankets, clothes, toys, and other materials – lack overall coordination leading to misplaced efforts, wasted resources, and logistical bottlenecks.

Another key distinction is between bilateral and multilateral development aid. As noted earlier, bilateral development aid is provided directly from one state to another, whereas multilateral development aid flows through various intermediaries, most often various *development finance institutions*. These organisations exist at different scales and work to promote development through the provision of financial – and technical – support. On a global scale, key development finance institutions include various components of the World Bank, including the International Bank for Reconstruction and Development (which was established in 1945 to support post-World War II recovery efforts), as well as the

International Development Agency, International Finance Corporation, and Multilateral Investment Guarantee Agency which support development finance in different ways.

In addition to the global-scale development finance institutions, an array of continental or regional multilateral development banks also play a key role in providing development financing. These include the African Development Bank, the Asian Development Bank, the Inter-American Development Bank, and the European Bank for Reconstruction and Development, as well as somewhat smaller banks including the European Investment Bank, Caribbean Development Bank, Development Bank of Southern Africa, Asian Infrastructure Investment Bank, and others.

TRADE OR AID?

One commonly promoted alternative to development aid is the call for 'trade not aid'. Often linked to neoliberalism, advocates for this approach argue that a market–based approach to development (in other words, free trade) is the best approach to support development, job creation, and market expansion while avoiding aid dependency. Broadly understood, the argument that growing trade is a more sustainable means of realising development outcomes focuses on the benefits of increased revenue through trade, reducing a country's trade deficit and (ideally) turning this into a trade surplus. In simple terms: if a country is spending more on imports than is earned on exports, they amass a trade deficit (which means the government may have to borrow money, taking on more debt and potentially limiting economic growth), whereas if a country earns more from exports than is spent on imports it gains an economic surplus that can be invested to further grow the economy.

This potential for economic growth, supporters argue, is evident in the success of the so-called 'Asian Tiger' economies which experienced rapid economic growth and development success through their exploitation of niches within the global market and rapid domination of these particular (often technological or financial sector) niches. However, as outlined in chapter 4, the success of the developmental state approach of many of these states relied upon a particular set of conditions that are not universal.

While growth in trade and exports can contribute to economic growth, critics highlight various limitations to this approach and argue that current global market and trade conditions perpetuate global inequalities and limit global development. The key questions that need to be asked then are: Who is trading what and to whom, and under what restrictions? The implementation of 'free-trade' agendas has led to an opening up of markets in the global south while allowing continued protectionist policies in the global north. In addition, the reliance upon a small number of primary commodity exports (such as coffee, cocoa, etc.) – with low 'value added' and profit margins – means many countries remain vulnerable to fluctuations in market demand and pricing.

This is particularly an issue for countries that are defined as having 'commodity dependence' – their economies are largely dependent upon (primary) commodity exports, a situation the UN and other bodies have long recognised as being linked to development challenges. This is a common situation for countries in the global south: in the 2000s and 2010s there were over 100 countries classed as having 'commodity dependence', all of which were based in the global south, with particular prominence in South America and sub-Saharan Africa. These conditions of dependence result from colonial policies, failures in post-independence policy environments to diversify economies, and global market and policy limitations. Crucially, this dependence can also contribute to 'rent seeking' behaviour and corruption, while leaving national economies vulnerable to price 'shocks' – such as the impacts on Ghana and Côte d'Ivoire (who produce over 60% of the world's cocoa) when cocoa prices dropped in the early 2000s.

THE EVOLVING LANDSCAPE OF DEVELOPMENT AID

Just as the overarching understandings of and approaches to development have changed over time, so too has the landscape of development aid. The dominance in policy circles of an emphasis on 'modernisation' and more recently 'neoliberalism' has led to particular forms of development aid flows – often linked to the promotion of self-sustained economic growth.

In the decades after the Second World War, two main sets of donors dominated the development aid arena during the Cold

War: the Development Assistance Committee (DAC) of the OECD (i.e. the West) and the Soviet-bloc-based Commission for Technical Assistance that operated within the Council for Mutual Economic Assistance (CMEA). As might be expected, these groupings strategically directed development aid and support to allies and proxies in the Cold War. With both sides in the Cold War seeking not only to maintain existing allies but also to expand their influence, it was common for military aid (including that for 'counter-insurgency' activities) to be a significant proportion of 'development' aid. Alongside military aid (including weapons, training, and other resources), donors would provide direct financial support and loans, as well as heavily subsidised resources – such as the Soviet Union's supplying of below-market-price oil to Cuba for both domestic use and resale on the world market (to generate hard currency revenue).

Elsewhere, Japanese aid in the post-World War II period was initially in the form of reparations that it was required to pay to 13 Asian countries ($2 billion up to 1977). On the back of these flows, Japanese companies and others recognised business opportunities in supporting development projects and loans, which set the foundations to subsequent bilateral aid relations with an array of states, with a focus primarily on industry and infrastructure development (Unger, 2018).

The collapse of the Soviet Union and the ending of the Cold War in the early 1990s led to a decrease in defence spending by many OECD countries. It had been hoped that this 'peace dividend' would be directed towards increased development aid spending. Instead, many OECD governments reduced their ODA spending as this was no longer needed for geopolitical and geostrategic reasons. In other words, as the need to build and maintain Cold War-era alliances faded, so too did the imperative to use development aid to foster these alliances. At the same time, many former recipients of support from CMEA found their development support – whether monetary or in the form of military aid or heavily subsidised oil imports – vanished.

While development aid flows and relations continued throughout the 1990s, campaigns to 'drop the debt' around the turn of the millennium and the introduction of the MDGs gave renewed impetus to and focus for ODA on quality-of-life concerns rather than macroeconomic reforms (Brown, 2014). These developments were linked to a growing recognition of the need for not only *more* but *better* aid – including removing 'tied aid' and increasing coordination of projects between donors. This concern with *better aid* led to the 2005 Paris Declaration on Aid Effectiveness and subsequent international summits including the 2008 Accra Agenda for Action and 2011 Busan Aid Effectiveness Summit.

WHY DO DONORS PROVIDE DEVELOPMENT FUNDING?

The drivers for 'giving' and 'receiving' are varied and changing, and related to the type of donor being discussed. While bi- and multilateral donors dominate the sector it is important to think about why philanthropists, companies, and individuals – including you, potentially – give money towards development initiatives. On these more individual levels, these actions may be values-driven (a desire to see greater equality, social justice, etc.), issues-driven (relating to environmental, ecological, health, education, etc.), guilt-driven, or rooted in familial or cultural norms and connections, but may also (cynics may suggest) be pragmatic choices relating to tax relief.

Corporate giving has a more 'patchy' reputation. Some companies are founded on ideals that commit them to supporting social, environmental, or other development agendas (Patagonia clothing for instance is a private, for-profit company which is now owned by a trust and non-profit organisation charged with using all profits towards tackling climate change and other environmental issues). Elsewhere prominent business people who have made fortunes in the commercial or finance sectors – such as Bill Gates, George Soros, and others – have committed vast sums to supporting global development. More often, however, major corporations strategically support or fund development initiatives as part of their 'corporate social responsibility' initiatives and are accused of 'greenwashing' their credentials through superficial (and ultimately self-interested) engagements with development issues.

SOUTH–SOUTH DEVELOPMENT COOPERATION

The development landscape is far more complex than the commonly assumed north–south donor–recipient relationship. One of the key alternative approaches has been cooperation between countries in 'the south' – a set of relations commonly called south–south development cooperation. While many talk of these as 'new' donors and relations, such an approach overlooks the histories of support and partnership between countries in the global south which pre-date the current development era (Mohan, 2016).

The origins of contemporary south–south development cooperation are often traced back to various summits and movements during the 1950s which sought to offer alternatives to the dominance of the global north and the East/West politics of the Cold War. At the 1955 Bandung Conference, independent African and Asian countries informally agreed to act as a bloc at the UN. Building from the Bandung Conference, the Non-Aligned Movement emerged as countries from the global south banded together to commit to non-interference and challenge the hegemony of the global north.

The subsequent creation of the Group of 77 by the nations who attended the UN Conference on Trade and Development in 1964 (originally comprising 77 countries, the G77 now numbers over 130 members) gave further impetus to these movements which act as an alternative to the G7 group of the most powerful economies. Responding to the continued economic (and political) dominance of the global north, the G77 called for a move to a New International Economic Order (NIEO). The principles of NIEO set out to tackle structural inequalities in trading relationships and provide more sovereign control over rights to natural resources and to nationalise vital industries.

Fundamentally these efforts coalesced around and promoted a vision of development rooted in solidarity and support between those on the peripheries of and disadvantaged by global political and economic systems, and resistance to global political and economic hegemony (Gray and Gills, 2016; Mohan, 2016). While south–south solidarity was increasingly marginalised by the debt crisis and rise of neoliberal orthodoxies in the 1970s, these links and ideals were not lost. Indeed, the G77 continued to identify south–south development cooperation as crucial for promoting economic independence, realising development, and ensuring an effective position within the global economic order. Throughout the later decades of the twentieth century and the opening years of the twenty-first century, numerous collaborations and mutual assistance programmes endured and recent years have seen a resurgence in the profile of south–south cooperation.

The language of 'mutual assistance' is often used to emphasise south–south solidarity and an ethos of mutuality which is located as different from the conditionalities and self-interest associated with 'traditional' aid relations. Often with an onus on skills and knowledge, these programmes may be quite small scale and focused on particular issues or sectors – from health to education to agriculture – but can also include major economic and infrastructural projects: from the Chinese funding of the Tazara Railway in the 1970s in East Africa, through to the myriad projects that comprise China's current Belt and Road Initiative. Elsewhere, the launching in 2001 of the New Partnership for Africa's Development (NEPAD) was positioned as inherently linked to south–south partnerships, offering 'African solutions to African problems' through both bi- and multi-lateral project support.

Amongst the most prominent forms of south–south development partnerships in the later parts of the twentieth century was Cuba's 'humanitarian internationalism' agenda. Following the success of the Cuban revolution in 1959, the Communist government pursued an ideology of internationalism that challenged the structural violence and underlying conditions of unequal development and human insecurity. Consequently, over many decades – and despite long-lasting, economically crippling US sanctions – Cuba strategically engaged in an array of south–south development partnerships, providing health, education, and military expertise and personnel to countries across Latin America and sub-Saharan Africa. Since the 1960s, Cuban 'medical brigades' comprising over 185,000 physicians have worked in over 100 countries, while over 25,000 medical students from the global south have studied at the island's Latin American Medical School. Alongside this, Cuban military support was prominent in a range of conflicts in sub-Saharan Africa – often framed as support for liberation struggles against colonialism and apartheid.

While the Cuban government may present this internationalist agenda as altruistic, the reality is that such engagements have a degree of self-interest: these partnerships provide important political capital (making 'friends' to support and protect you) as well as being a vital source of financial capital (many agreements involve payments by the recipient countries both to the individuals involved (i.e. paying doctors' salaries) as well as to the Cuban government (which receives the tax revenues levied on the salaries of Cuban doctors working in South Africa)).

In recent years, a number of countries in the global south have emerged as increasingly significant players in the world economy. From the economic success of the 'Asian Tigers' to the economic growth of Brazil, Russia, India, China, and (to a lesser extent) South Africa (known as the BRICS), growing economic success and confidence have led to a strengthening of south–south development cooperation. As noted earlier, the drivers for these collaborations are multiple, including the desire to escape the bonds of colonial history and associated power dynamics, the relative lack of conditionalities to partnerships and funding, as well as strategic efforts to develop geopolitical alliances and 'soft' political capital and access to strategic mineral, energy, agricultural, trade, geostrategic, and other resources. Thus, while decolonialism, equality, and solidarity remain professed as key tenets of such partnerships, the realities are more complex, infused with economic and political (self-)interest. In recent years, we have seen the increasing power and influence of India and – in particular – China in these south–south partnerships. As explored in the next section, the growing prominence of so-called 'new donors' such as China and India contributes to an evolving balance of power within the development aid landscape.

NEW DONORS AND RECIPIENT-DONORS

Linked to the expansion of south–south development partnerships, there has been growing recognition of the diversity and power of a raft of so-called 'new' donors. These 'new' donors are not necessarily new at all; many of these states have long histories of providing regional and/or global development cooperation and support. Instead, what is 'new' is Western political and popular awareness – and, ultimately, concerns that the non-DAC donors are increasingly able to operate in ways that disrupt entrenched landscapes of development finance that have been dominated by a small number of Western donors and International Financial

Institutions (IFIs). It is important to recognise here that this shifting landscape is not only about bilateral and state-provided development aid, but also the emergence of alternatives such as the New Development Bank and the China-led Asian Infrastructure Investment Bank that can offer concessionary loans and thus offer a different option to the World Bank and the IMF.

Driving the popularity (amongst recipient states) of 'new' donors is the relative freedom from conditionalities and other ties or constraints – either in what monies can be used for, or in relation to required changes to policy and practice. In recent years this is perhaps most clearly seen in the split between efforts by OECD-linked donors to promote good governance and social inclusion, whereas 'new' donors place far less emphasis on these concerns and instead are focused on supporting in-country economic growth and infrastructure development (Mawdsley, 2014).

These 'new' donors typically include countries located in the global south, as well as Central and Eastern European, and Gulf states. Most prominent within these states are China, India, Brazil, Turkey, but also countries such as Thailand, Azerbaijan, Nigeria, Gabon, and others – all of whom are involved in providing support to both longer-term development projects and emergency relief. The role of such non-DAC donors has been growing – from a historic low of 5% of global ODA-like flows in the late 1990s to 15%–20% in the early 2010s (Mawdsley, 2017). As with DAC countries, the development partnerships and practices are bound up in both recipient needs and donor self-interest, with non-DAC donors often seeking resource and energy security, market access, and soft political power. On the flip side, the lack of conditionalities amongst other factors means that for recipients, even if support is in the form of tied aid, the lower transaction, exchange, and labour/material costs mean that non-DAC donor funding goes further (i.e. it offers better value for money). However, the domestic political agendas and historical experiences of non-DAC donors shape their aid practices *and* the ways in which they are viewed by recipients. Simultaneously, the types of development cooperation provided by 'new' donors often encompass more than OECD-defined ODA, which can blur boundaries of geopolitical and strategic interests (e.g. resource access).

The donor landscape, as we have seen, is not static – and this dynamism is perhaps most evident in the shifting role of middle-income countries (MICs) such as Brazil, Turkey, India, Nigeria, and Pakistan. Why are such countries of particular interest here? The answer is this: such states are often both donors and recipients of international development support. Following a prolonged period of global economic growth, a significant number of countries have moved from the World Bank definition of 'low-income' to now being 'middle-income' countries. For critics, this move to being 'middle-income' and, potentially, a donor country with greater domestic economic resources and access to global financial flows, means that their need for development support is marginal. In recent years, the tabloid press in the UK have seized upon these narratives in questioning why the UK still provides ODA to India for instance. However, such a simplistic approach overlooks not only the vast range of countries classified as MIC – there are over 100 MICs, from Vanuatu to China, Indonesia to Tuvalu, with GNI per capita figures of between $1,000 and $12,000 – and the range of development concerns and challenges facing each of these, but also the legacies of (infra)structural deficits and other vulnerabilities.

Alonso et al. (2016) argue that these MICs – who are, or may become, donor-recipient states – are vital to the realisation of the SDGs. On the one hand, such states require continued development support to overcome bottlenecks, tackle technical and productive changes, and address energy and environmental issues as well as levels of persistent poverty and domestic inequality. On the other, they can also play a pivotal role in facilitating south–south development cooperation, providing cheaper and more appropriate technical assistance, and supporting the realisation of regional 'public goods' and development goals.

THE ROLE OF CHINA

Amongst the 'new' donors, the most prominent and controversial actor is China. Given China's increasing economic and political engagement with low- and middle-income countries – particularly in Africa – various of the controversies and concerns that have been raised with this new-found prominence relate also to broader economic engagements. Since 1996 Chinese investment in Africa – backed by foreign currency and political support in Beijing – has grown rapidly, starting with oil exploration and extraction but including copper and iron ore mines, timber, mineral mining, and other industries. These investments have encouraged a 'look East' policy amongst many African political leaders who, in turn, have benefited from the material, infrastructural, and economic benefits of Chinese investment. While these investments have led to the building of new sports stadia, roads, railways, and other infrastructure, critics have cautioned that the costs incurred – through loans and the like – risk African states becoming, in essence, mortgaged to the Chinese state, banks, and other financial institutions. Other concerns focus on profit extraction by Chinese firms, the numbers of Chinese workers and labourers who were brought to African countries to complete projects while local workers remained unemployed, and the discarding of environmental and labour standards.

Development aid flows from China are sometimes termed 'rogue aid' by Western commentators who argue that Chinese development finance is far from altruistic but instead is driven by political and economic self-interest. Critics of Western-led development approaches have noted the irony of these charges, noting how development aid from DAC throughout the 1950s through to the early years of the twenty-first century was often also driven by donor agendas and (geo)political interests and statesmanship (Dreher and Fuchs, 2015). Contemporary concerns with China's 'rogue aid' remain focused upon whether/the extent to which the donor is prioritising their own benefits rather than those of the recipient; put very bluntly and provocatively: To what extent can China's development links be understood as a genuine form of south–south development cooperation, or are these a new form of extractivism and exploitation?

Alongside these concerns, further criticisms are levelled that the lack of conditionalities imposed by new donors on development finance, and a lower emphasis on human rights, environmental protection, and working conditions, are undermining global efforts towards good governance and human rights. On the flip side, China uses this mantra or principle of non-interference in a recipient state's internal and sovereign affairs as a cornerstone of development and foreign policy (Dreher and Fuchs, 2015). As a result, many states now view China as the development funder/lender of choice (Malik et al., 2021).

While Western interest in China's aid policy has peaked in recent years due to clear geo-political, -strategic, and -economic manoeuvring by China (which is seen in the West as a threat to the established geopolitical order), China has a much longer history of providing development finance. In the 1950s, China began providing assistance to North Korea as well as offering grants and interest-free loans to a small number of countries in Africa, the Arabian peninsula, and China's immediate neighbours. This development finance was often targeted to support independence and anti-colonial movements in these states. China rapidly expanded overseas aid provision during the 1970s under Chairman Mao Zedong's drive to position China as the political leader for the global south. This period also saw a move away from major projects and towards support for smaller-scale projects, mutually beneficial trade agreements, and a reduction in grants and interest-free loans.

Following the 1989 Tiananmen Square student-led protests and massacre by state security forces, China resorted to 'chequebook diplomacy' to try to (re)gain support and international standing. As a result, development aid was increased – particularly to African and Latin American states. By the late 1990s, China's focus shifted again towards a more market-orientated approach to development aid, and diversification of funding types and recipients (Dreher and Fuchs, 2015). Over the past 20 years or so, Chinese international development funding has risen from $32 billion per year to $85 billion per year – more than double that of the US and other major bilateral donors (Malik et al., 2021). This financing, however, was predominantly provided as loans rather than grants (roughly $82.5 billion provided as loans, compared to approximately $2.5 billion in grants), meaning many now view China as a de facto banker rather than benefactor (Malik et al., 2021: 1) – with increasing amounts of this financing provided through state-owned commercial banks. Between 2000 and 2017, the main recipients of ODA from China were Iraq ($8.15 billion), DPRK ($7.17 billion), Ethiopia ($6.57 billion), Indonesia ($4.42 billion), and Congo ($4.24 billion); figures dwarfed by the amounts provided through semi- or non-concessional loans (known as Other Official Finance or OOF) to Russia ($125.38 billion), Venezuela ($85.54 billion), Angola ($40.65 billion), Brazil ($39.08 billion), and Kazakhstan ($39.01 billion) (Malik et al., 2021: 19). This volume of financing has led to over 40 low- and middle-income countries carrying a debt exposure to China of at least 10% of their GDP, often with these debts guaranteed against the recipient state's future export earnings (Malik et al., 2021: 1).

The most recent evolution in China's global development involvement is the hugely ambitious Belt and Road Initiative (BRI). Launched in 2013, this initiative represents China's attempt to not only enhance global connectivity but crucially access to resources and cement the role of China as a global superpower. Involving almost 1,000 projects and hundreds of billions of dollars of funding across 140 countries, advocates for the BRI claim this as an example of south–south cooperation that provides low- and middle-income countries with an alternative pathway to development (Malik et al., 2021: 3). Critics of the BRI have raised concerns that China may be overexposing its economy (and commercial banks) to debt, that many recipient states are at risk of falling into unsustainable debts (and risking then becoming beholden to China), and that the BRI initiative is primarily a mechanism through which China hopes to boost its own global standing more than focusing upon the development outcomes in other states.

REMITTANCES AND HOME-TOWN ASSOCIATIONS

Remittances have become a key source of foreign income for many countries in the global south, as migrant workers send money or goods to support their families, communities, or home-towns. As these flows of resources happen in various ways – including bank transfers, wire transfers with Western Union or other companies, the shipping or carrying of goods or physical cash, etc. – it is impossible to know the total value of remittances sent in any one year. However, the IMF estimated that by 2017 officially recorded remittance flows would total $596 billion – of which $450 billion was moving to economies in the global south – with another $900 billion of remittances via informal flows (Ratha, 2005). For low-income countries, these flows might account for 4% of their GDP (Ratha, 2005), and the World Bank has estimated that in the early 2000s remittances led to a reduction in household poverty by 11% in Uganda and 6% in Bangladesh.

Over recent decades the amount of remittances being sent (in $ terms) has grown significantly, becoming a key source of funding for households and livelihoods as well as meeting or supporting local development needs and projects. Growing recognition of the contribution of remittances to development outcomes is reflected in the inclusion of specific targets within migration-related SDG indicators 10.c.1 and 10.7.1 (reducing costs of remittances and recruitment costs for migrant workers) and 17.3.2 (increasing volume of remittances as percentage of GDP). Furthermore, the importance of these flows is illustrated when we compare these to monies provided through both ODA and FDI – in 2000, financial flows to developing countries comprised 18% ODA, 23% remittances, and 59% non-ODA monies; in 2015 these figures were 17% ODA, 35% remittances, and 48% non-ODA (Overton and Murray, 2021: 7). Then, in 2020, for the first time, remittance flows ($540 billion) exceeded the combined flows from FDI ($259 billion) and ODA ($179 billion) (Ratha et al., 2021).

The majority of remittances are sent person-to-person, typically within family or household relations, and these *private* flows are typically used to pay for basic needs, educational or health costs, housing and land, as well as to support small business enterprises – as well as having knock-on effects in relation to tax revenues and other benefits for national economies. These can have hugely beneficial impacts on household income, poverty reduction, and investments in future generations but may not support *public goods* such as infrastructural development and other national developmental priorities (Mercer and Page, 2014). Whether for private or public goods, the costs of sending remittances through formal channels remain notably above the 3% cost target set out in SDG 10.c.1. At present, the average cost for sending a remittance of $200 to a low-/middle-income country is 6.58% – although this varies by region, from 4.9% to South Asia to 8.2% in sub-Saharan Africa (https://www.migrationdataportal.org/themes/remittances). With remittance flows in the billions of dollars per year, these costs and charges are sizable and provide a key drain upon and limitation on remittance flows and development outcomes.

As Table 6.2 illustrates, remittance flows were increasing up until 2019 – when the Covid-19 pandemic severely curtailed international travel and caused huge economic slowdown and

Table 6.2 Remittance flows to low- and middle-income regions in $billions

Region	2009	2016	2019	2020*	2022**
Low- and middle-income	302	441	548	540	565
East Asia & Pacific	80	128	148	136	142
Europe & Central Asia	33	43	62	56	50
Latin America (incl. Caribbean)	55	73	96	103	112
Middle East & North Africa	31	49	55	56	59
South Asia	75	111	140	147	158
Sub-Saharan Africa	28	37	48	42	44
World	433	597	719	702	726

Source: Ratha et al. (2021: 3)

Notes: World Bank data include the salaries of temporary migrant workers, even though not all of this will be remitted; *estimated, **forecast

drastic increases in unemployment. This drop in remittance flows in 2019 was a crucial challenge for many, not only for individual households dependent upon these flows to meet basic survival needs but also for national economies where remittances account for a significant percentage of GDP (e.g. 38% for Tonga, 33% for Lebanon) – a situation exacerbated during Covid where health and other care costs spiked, while FDI, tourism revenue, and other income streams declined and economies shrank. Interestingly, the World Bank had expected global remittance flows to drop to $508 billion in 2020 and $470 billion in 2021 due to Covid-19 (Ratha et al., 2021). While the data paint a far more positive picture, these higher than expected flows reflect an enforced move from informal (i.e. hand-carrying of money) to formal (i.e. wire or bank transfers) channels of remittances due to travel restrictions. As a result, the real-terms drop in remittances may be far higher than is indicated here.

Looking beyond the regional data (Table 6.2), the top recipient countries of remittances in cash terms in 2020 were India ($83 billion), China ($60 billion), Mexico ($43 billion), Philippines ($35 billion), and Egypt ($30 billion). Meanwhile, the top recipient countries in terms of percentage of GDP have far smaller national economies, leading to greater risks of dependency on and vulnerability to disruptions to remittance flows (such as the 2009 global financial crisis or the more recent Covid-19 pandemic). Specifically, these were Tonga (38%), Lebanon (33%), Kyrgyzstan (29%), Tajikistan (27%), and El Salvador, Honduras, and Nepal (all at 24%).

So we have a sense of where the main recipients are, but where do these remittances come from? Unsurprisingly, the main sources for remittances are those states with larger economies and a significant presence of immigrants – whether temporary workers, undeclared migrants, formal migrants, or second- or third-generation immigrants. You may well have guessed (correctly) that the US is the largest source of remittances ($68 billion of outflows), but perhaps you are less likely to have guessed the next two: the United Arab Emirates ($43 billion) and Saudi Arabia ($35 billion) (Ratha et al., 2021: 6). If these figures are a surprise, it is worth noting that of the estimated 281 million migrants (including refugees) in 2020 (Ratha et al., 2021: 6), the countries hosting the largest numbers of migrants were the US (51 million), Germany (16 million), Saudi Arabia (13 million), Russia (12 million), and the UK, France, and UAE (9 million each).

It should also be noted that remittances and flows of money, knowledge, and other support within families or through small-scale development partnerships between members of the diaspora (those who have migrated overseas, but retaining a sense of connection to their place of birth) and their home-towns are increasingly important. Despite states historically being distrustful of emigrants and diaspora organisations, in recent years many countries in the global south have begun to proactively build relations with their diaspora communities and support or facilitate their role in supporting local development initiatives. Indeed, policy interest in the role of diaspora in supporting development has increased swiftly in recent years, including efforts to encourage the formalisation of remittance flows or to mobilise the wealth – rather than income – of diasporas through new financial products (Mercer and Page, 2014).

Home-Town Associations (HTAs) and other collective organisations amongst diasporas have a long history, providing social, professional, and other networks and support. HTAs – organisations for migrants from a particular town or region – initially emerged to support members of the diaspora but are increasingly involved in the collection and raising of funds to support collective development projects in the home-town. These projects are often infrastructural (support for the provision of clean water, road improvements, etc.) or service-related (related to health-care or education for instance) (Mercer and Page, 2014). Recognising the potential role of HTAs in promoting development, various national governments have sought to engage with these groups and incentivise their development/fundraising activities – such as Mexico's 3x1 initiative, whereby for each $1 raised and remitted by HTAs another $3 are provided by the government (Mercer and Page, 2014). Concerns remain over the potential for the diaspora to perpetuate local conflicts and ferment dissent or disruption, and their remittances may also entrench existing inequalities at different scales, cause potential mismatch between the HTA's vision for development activities and national/local government priorities, and may lead to reliance upon remittances to fund development projects – with the assumption that these will continue (Mercer and Page, 2014).

PHILANTHROPY, FAIR TRADE, AND 'BRAND-AID'

Alongside key ODA flows, other notable forms of financial support for development are seen in the differing ways in which individuals make decisions to support global development. This may be through charitable giving and philanthropy (where individuals, companies, or other entities provide monetary support to a charitable organisation or appeal – be this Oxfam, Water Aid, or the Disaster Emergencies Committee for instance; or the role of organisations such as the Ford Foundation or Bill and Melinda Gates Foundation) or voluntourism (where individuals or groups spend time 'doing' development work – typically this is in an overseas (usually global south) country; see Jacob, 2019; Wearing et al., 2018). It may also be through 'consumer' choices and purchasing of 'fair trade' certified products (meaning the producers are paid a 'fair' wage and may receive other social benefits funded through this premium) or 'Brand-Aid' products (such as Product Red).

Philanthropic giving has been a longstanding development finance stream, drawing upon both mass donations and appeals as well as the largesse of wealthy individuals. Amongst the more prominent philanthropic organisations are the Ford Foundation, MacArthur Foundation, and Rockefeller Foundation as well as more recent ones including Bill and Melinda Gates Foundation and Open Society Foundation.

These foundations provide billions of dollars of support each year: founded by billionaire George Soros, the Open Society Foundation has spent over $18 billion since the 1990s ($1.4 billion in 2020 alone) to promote inclusive democracies and governmental accountability across the globe. The Bill and Melinda Gates Foundation has, since being established in 2000, become one of the largest charitable foundations in the world with over 1,600 employees and a $50 billion endowment to support social, health, education, and other development projects. Both the Ford Foundation (established in 1936) and MacArthur Foundation provide hundreds of millions of dollars a year in development grants. On a smaller scale, the Oprah Winfrey Charitable Foundation has donated $400 million primarily to support educational initiatives, while Dietmar Hopp – the founder of the Dietmar Hopp Stiftung organisation – has donated over $1 billion in support to health, community, and education projects in Germany (you can find accessible information on various philanthropists here: http://www.philanthropic-giving.com/).

While the total amounts provided through philanthropic giving are dwarfed by formal ODA (the World Bank estimated that in 2005 $4.5 billion was provided via international philanthropy, compared with $100 billion of ODA from OECD countries (Moran and Stone, 2016)), this support is seen as vital in filling gaps in provision from state, market, and bi- and multilateral support. In addition, philanthropic giving and engagement are also recognised as integral to shaping policy and both popular and political attitudes and priorities (Moran and Stone, 2016).

At the same time, however, philanthropy is criticised on various levels. Writing in the 1990s, post-development scholar Arturo Escobar (1995) argued that the drive to philanthropy was part of an agenda to 'modernise poverty', turning the 'poor' into the 'assisted' – a category of people viewed as a social problem and requiring new forms of (social) control and intervention. Other critiques include the continued dominance of development priorities – and therefore funding allocations – by philanthropic 'givers' in the global north and questions over the effectiveness and negative impacts of 'venture philanthropy' (investing monies and using the profits on these for charitable causes) on the very development challenges philanthropists are seeking to address.

Alongside a growth in philanthropic giving, recent years have also seen a growth in consumer-based 'giving'. This commonly occurs in two ways: fairtrade and 'Brand Aid' (Ponte and Richey, 2014). Fairtrade is, as it sounds, a commitment to and recognition of trade that is done in a 'fair' manner. The roots of this movement in the UK date to the 1960s as a grassroots political statement against dominant geopolitical norms and exploitative global trading relationships. Over the past 60 years, the movement has expanded to cover a wider range of countries and products, to the extent that Fairtrade has moved from a radical, niche market to a staple in many mainstream supermarkets and stores and with schools, universities, towns/cities, and even countries committing to sourcing and using fairtrade products in order to be certified as Fairtrade.

Most commonly this is encountered through the Fairtrade certification and labelling of products including bananas, coffee, chocolate, tea, and so on. Overseen by an international body, fairtrade certification shows that various environmental, labour, social, and other standards have been met by producers and traders and that fair trade producers are provided with a 'social premium' to support local development projects. How this premium – which means the price to consumers of fairtrade goods is generally higher – is used is determined by the fairtrade-certified collectives of producers/growers; typically it is used to support improvements to local infrastructure, health, and education provision. Supporters of fairtrade point to the reach of this movement, with almost 2 million farmers and workers worldwide linked to 1,800 certified producers each benefitting from a share of the almost £170 million of fairtrade premiums distributed in 2020 (Fairtrade, 2022). However, critics have challenged the success of fairtrade schemes for failing to ensure enough of the social premium reaches the growers and producers, arguing that too much of the premium is consumed in overheads, certification fees, or ineffectively used by cooperative leaderships.

The term Brand Aid refers to the consumer-focused means of supporting global development based upon the power of consumption as a means of achieving both development outcomes and a sense of personal well-being, all promoted by celebrity endorsement. This trend is a clear part of the rise of 'glamour aid' – as Moyo (2009) terms it – during the start of the twenty-first century. The increasing role and prominence of celebrity in global development campaigns has been notable (see also chapter 5). Other terms used to describe these efforts include cause marketing or cause-related marketing.

One obvious example of Brand Aid is Product Red (often presented as (PRODUCT)^{RED} or (PRODUCT)RED). Founded in 2006, with initial promotional campaigns featuring Bono and other celebrities, (RED) invite you to buy co-branded products to raise money for good causes overseas. You can 'shop (RED) save lives' by buying yourself a Product(RED) iPhone, iPhone cover, or Apple Watch, Montblanc trolley case, Beats headphones, Durex condoms, or even a Vespa scooter or RAM pick-up truck.

Yep, that's right – you too can feel amazing about yourself, look cool, and gain social prestige while at the same time supporting the Global Fund to fight HIV/AIDS, TB, and Malaria, or supporting another development initiative. All you do is buy this co-branded laptop, pair of shoes, sunglasses, T-shirt, headphones, etc. Heck, (RED) will even support your 'repping' it on social media – boost those likes! Sounds simple? You buy something – perhaps at a slightly inflated price – and the purchase means a donation is made to a global development cause. Win-win, surely?

Well, not entirely. Yes, such projects can deliver benefits: by late 2021, the (RED) website proclaimed that they had impacted 220 million lives, raised $650 million for the Global Fund, and supported 15 countries. At the same time, critics caution that such practices can depoliticise development and mask the structural factors behind power and inequality, and may be cynically viewed as an effort at corporate and celebrity branding. Others have cautioned that Brand Aid initiatives encourage a specific, consumption-orientated approach to giving – an approach which sits uneasily in relation to growing sustainability pressures. Such approaches also often reinforce the power dynamics and representational practices which locate who and where the 'needy' are – and, crucially, this 'needy-ness' is commodified, branded, and marketed to Western consumers, who can then 'save' the day (Ponte and Richey, 2014).

DEVELOPMENT AID ON THE GROUND

Development aid is clearly neither an unmitigated 'good' nor a 'magic bullet' to realise equitable global development. As this chapter has explored, development aid is often linked to geopolitical (self)interest, infused with (economic) ideologies, and laden with power. Valid concerns remain with the potential for ODA to contribute to continued dependency and facilitate new forms of neo-colonialism, challenges of corruption, and ineffective and inefficient coordination and use of development aid between donors and recipients. However, the fierce opposition to development aid from some neoliberal commentators seems excessive, reflecting a continued (and flawed) belief in the power of the market and of trickle-down economics.

On the ground, development aid can have vital, life-saving, and life-altering impacts and benefits. However, the continued dominance of development relationships by donors means that interventions and aid spending do not always address the most pressing local needs. Indeed, the shifting of strategic priorities by donors and time limits on spending cycles can result in inefficiencies. For instance, budgets may need to be spent within a particular time period (often 12 months) which can lead to donors and others rushing to spend monies at the end of an annual reporting period.

For recipients, especially NGOs and CSOs that rely upon ODA support to function, the need to continually apply for funding and to adjust and adapt to shifting donor priorities leads to key challenges with the recruitment and retention of skilled staff, excessive time spent on applications, and reorienting strategic goals and missions. At the same time, international donor community efforts in recent years to bypass national governments and provide ODA directly to NGOs and CSOs – including in relation to the current 'good governance' agenda – have led, in a number of contexts, to growing suspicion towards NGOs and increased restrictions on their space to function. Often couched in language of 'professionalising' NGOs and ensuring accountability and transparency, various national governments have enacted restrictive measures relating to the registration and operations of NGOs and – crucially – where they can source funding from, as witnessed in India, Zimbabwe, Rwanda, or Uganda. Additionally, critics have argued that the use of local NGOs by international donors as service delivery agents is further exacerbating tensions over the (expected) role of NGOs within different national contexts. Historically, NGOs have played a variety of roles – from activism and advocacy, through being watchdogs upon state power, to being supporters of the state, or partners in service delivery. However, these dynamics appear to be changing – with decreasing spaces for activism and advocacy, and a growing focus upon NGOs as service delivery partners.

REFERENCES

Alonso, J.A., Glennie, J., Sumner, A. (2016). Recipients and contributors: The dual role of middle-income countries. In Grugel, J., Hammett, D. (eds) *The Palgrave Handbook of International Development* (pp. 315–332). London: Palgrave Macmillan.

Banerjee, A.V., Duflo, E. (2011). *Poor Economics: A Radical Rethinking of the Way to Fight Global Poverty*. New York: Public Affairs.

Brown, S. (2014) Foreign aid in a changing world. In Desai, V., Potter, R. (eds) *The Companion to Development Studies* (pp. 539–542). Abingdon: Routledge.

Cosgrove, S., Curtis, B. (2018). *Understanding Global Poverty: Causes, Capabilities and Human Development*. Abingdon: Routledge.

Degnbol-Martinussen, J., Engberg-Pedersen, P. (2003). *Aid: Understanding International Development Cooperation*. London: Zed Books.

Donortracker (2022). Donor profile: US. Berlin: SEEK Development. https://donortracker.org/country/united-states (retrieved 17/09/2022).

Dreher, A., Fuchs, A. (2015). Rogue aid? An empirical analysis of China's aid allocation. *Canadian Journal of Economics*, 48 (3): 988–1023.

Dreher, A., Fuchs, A., Nunnenkamp, P. (2013). New donors. *International Interactions*, 39 (3): 402–415.

Escobar, A. (1995). *Encountering Development: The Making and Unmaking of the Third World*. Princeton, NJ: Princeton University Press.

Fairtrade (2022). Facts and figures about Fairtrade. London: Fairtrade Foundation. https://www.fairtrade.org.uk/what-is-fairtrade/facts-and-figures-about-fairtrade/ (retrieved 02/12/2022).

Ganga, P., Girod, D. (2019). Ties that bind: The impact of tied aid on development. IPES Paper.

Goldin, I. (2018). *Development: A Very Short Introduction*. Oxford: Oxford University Press.

Gray, K., Gills, B.K. (2016). South–South cooperation and the rise of the Global South. *Third World Quarterly*, 37 (4): 557–574.

Jacob, H. (2019). The unspeakable whiteness of volunteer tourism. *Annals of Tourism Research*, 76: 326–327.

Malik, A., Parks, B., Russell, B., Lin, J., Walsh, K., Solomon, K., Zhang, S., Elston, T., Goodman, S. (2021). *Banking on the Belt and Road: Insights from a New Global Dataset of 13,427 Chinese Development Projects*. Williamsburg, VA: AidData at William & Mary.

Mawdsley, E. (2014). The rising powers as development donors and partners. In Desai, V., Potter, R. (eds) *The Companion to Development Studies* (pp. 543–546). Abingdon: Routledge.

Mawdsley, E. (2017). Development geography I: Cooperation, competition and convergence between 'North' and 'South'. *Progress in Human Geography*, 41 (1): 108–117.

Mercer, C., Page, B. (2014). Diaspora and development. In Desai, V., Potter, R. (eds) *The Companion to Development Studies* (pp. 217–222). Abingdon: Routledge.

Mohan, G. (2016). Emerging powers in international development: Questioning south-south cooperation. In Grugel, J., Hammett, D. (eds) *The Palgrave Handbook of International Development* (pp. 279–296). London: Palgrave Macmillan.

Moran, M., Stone, D. (2016). The new philanthropy: Private power in international development policy? In Grugel, J., Hammett, D. (eds) *The Palgrave Handbook of International Development* (pp. 297–313). London: Palgrave Macmillan.

Moyo, D. (2009). *Dead Aid: Why Aid is Not Working and How There is Another Way for Africa*. London: Penguin.

OECD (2022). Official development assistance (ODA). Paris: OECD. https://www.oecd.org/dac/financing-sustainable-development/development-finance-standards/official-development-assistance.htm (retrieved 15/10/2022).

OECD.Stat (2022). Aid (ODA) disbursements to countries and regions [DAC2a]. Paris: OECD. https://stats.oecd.org/Index.aspx?DataSetCode=TABLE2A (retrieved 18/11/2022).

O'Keefe, P., Rose, J. (2014). Humanitarian aid. In Desai, V., Potter, R. (eds) *The Companion to Development Studies* (pp. 507–512). Abingdon: Routledge.

Overton, J., Murray, W. (2021). *Aid and Development*. Abingdon: Routledge.

Ponte, S., Richey, L.A. (2014). Buying into development? Brand Aid forms of cause-related marketing. *Third World Quarterly*, 35 (1): 65–87.

Ratha, D. (2005). What are remittances? *Finance & Development*, 42 (4): 76–77. https://www.imf.org/external/pubs/ft/fandd/basics/76-remittances.htm (retrieved 10/05/2022).

Ratha, D., Kim, E.J., Plaza, S., Seshan, G. (2021). *Migration and Development Brief 34: Resilience: COVID-19 Crisis through a Migration Lens*. Washington, DC: KNOMAD-World Bank.

Serieux, J. (2018). Aid and debt. In Binns, T., Lynch, K., Nel, E. (eds) *The Routledge Handbook of African Development* (pp. 327–340). Abingdon: Routledge.

Unger, C. (2018). *International Development: A Postwar History*. London: Bloomsbury Academic.

Wearing, S., Mostafanezhad, M., Nguyen, N., Nguyen, T.H.T., McDonald, M. (2018). 'Poor children on Tinder' and their Barbie Saviours: Towards a feminist political economy of volunteer tourism. *Leisure Studies*, 37 (5): 500–514.

IS THERE A FUTURE FOR GLOBAL DEVELOPMENT?

The question of whether there is a future for global development or not depends, perhaps entirely, on whether there is a future for humanity on planet earth. Arguably, realising just and sustainable global development is crucial to ensuring there is a habitable planet for future generations. The key consideration then is, what does the future of global development look like?

As this book has argued, we cannot understand the current global development landscape without examining its history. Likewise, we cannot begin to predict the future of global development without remembering this past and learning from it. The legacies of Empire and colonialism continue to permeate global development in multiple ways. The dominance of institutions, knowledges, and power based in the global north has led to particular understandings of and approaches to global development, many of which have served to perpetuate inequalities at multiple scales. With the apparent failures of Western-led development and aid strategies, it is unsurprising that critics have questioned the future of global development and challenged the foundations of the sector as being rooted in imperialism, racism, and self-interest (Moyo, 2009).

In light of such critiques, what is the future likely to hold for global development? During the writing of this book, the UK has experienced its hottest year on record, while the Russian invasion of Ukraine is contributing to global food shortages, hunger, and soaring food and fuel prices, is consuming vast amounts of financial and material resources, and is releasing vast amounts of greenhouse gases, all while causing extensive human suffering and driving

DOI: 10.4324/9781003155652-7

migration flows. Meanwhile, the British government is pushing ahead with its efforts to offshore asylum seekers for processing in Rwanda, while global migration flows continue to grow. Recent reports have highlighted that global inequalities are worsening – exacerbated by the Covid-19 pandemic – not only in terms of wealth and income, but also in access to health-care, Covid-19 vaccines, carbon emissions, and on and on the list goes.

In the face of such a daunting set of challenges – some fundamental to the very survival of human life on the planet – what might be the priorities for global development? The obvious place to start is with the SDGs.

WILL WE REALISE THE SDGS BY 2030?

The short answer is no.

The slightly longer answer is that some countries will meet some of the targets by 2030, but the majority of targets are likely to be missed.

Of the 169 SDG targets, 21 should have been met by the end of 2020. Of these, only three had been realised (to conserve at least 10% of coastal and marine areas; develop and operationalise a global strategy for youth employment; increase access to ICTs), while six had seen zero progress or had actually moved further away from the target. Looking ahead to other targets to be met between now and 2030, there has been important progress towards improving child and maternal health outcomes, access to electricity, and several other indicators. However, major challenges remain including persistent inequalities, rising numbers living in extreme poverty, and the accelerating impacts of climate change – challenges which seem insurmountable with current policy approaches. Indeed, as food and fuel prices rise across the globe, concerns grow of a potential global recession, and national budgets are squeezed further, progress towards meeting many of the SDG targets is looking increasingly challenging.

Given the increasing pressures from climate change and the strong likelihood of our failure to meet the SDG targets, two questions need addressing. First, what are the main priorities which will need addressing beyond 2030? And, second, do we need a much more radical approach to realising *sustainable* global development?

GLOBAL DEVELOPMENT PRIORITIES

Global development concerns are, inherently, entangled with each other. This makes identifying key priorities difficult. Nonetheless, there are various key areas which are clearly of concern.

CLIMATE CHANGE

Our changing climate is, despite the efforts of climate denialists to suggest otherwise, clearly wreaking huge havoc on the world already. Recent years have seen records being broken for hottest or driest days, weeks, months, and years with increasing frequency, the intensity and frequency of extreme weather events and wild-fires increase, sea-levels inexorably rise, and productive lands being lost to desertification. The 2022 Intergovernmental Panel on Climate Change report emphasises these concerns, stating that we are very close to or may have already passed crucial environmental tipping points (IPCC, 2022). The planet is, in short, burning – and any sustainable future for not only global development but humanity requires urgent action to address global warming and climate change.

In other words, the need for sustainable global development is more urgently apparent now than when the Brundtland Commission Report was released. The crucial challenge is, how do we look to meet the needs of the present without jeopardising the abilities of future generations? This requires a fundamental rethinking not only of what we understand development to be and how it is measured, but of the underlying (and inherently destructive) capitalist logic of accumulation and consumption.

More immediately, and in keeping with widespread scientific consensus, there is a need to rapidly – and permanently – reduce emissions of greenhouse gases (including carbon dioxide and methane). Despite overwhelming evidence, why is progress to this end so slow? To put it bluntly, political leaders are prioritising national and short-term political self-interest (leaders are wary of committing to policies with short-term economic costs – which may cost them and their party at the next election – and ill-defined or unquantifiable longer-term benefits). Understandably, the leaders of countries in the global south have argued that states in the global north need to take the lead in tackling carbon emissions and provide support and redress to states in the global south. These claims recognise inequalities in carbon emissions, both historic and contemporary. Historical emissions linked to carbon-intensive industrial revolutions and economic growth in the global north are thought to have contributed 64% of energy-related CO_2 emissions since 1850, compared with 34% for middle-income countries and 2% for low-income countries over the same time period (Bierbaum et al., 2010). These disparities remain evident in the present, with the UN (2019: 17) estimating that 'the top 10 per cent of emitters contribute to about 45 per cent of global carbon dioxide emissions, while the bottom 50 per cent of emitters contribute to 13 per cent of global emissions' (also see Figure 7.1). Meanwhile, the biggest impacts of and costs associated with climate change are being experienced in the

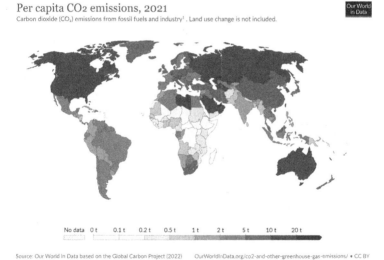

Per capita CO_2 emissions, 2021
Carbon dioxide (CO_2) emissions from fossil fuels and industry[1] . Land use change is not included.

No data   0 t   0.1 t   0.2 t   0.5 t   1 t   2 t   5 t   10 t   20 t

Source: Our World in Data based on the Global Carbon Project (2022)   OurWorldInData.org/co2-and-other-greenhouse-gas-emissions/ • CC BY

1. **Fossil emissions:** Fossil emissions measure the quantity of carbon dioxide (CO_2) emitted from the burning of fossil fuels, and directly from industrial processes such as cement and steel production. Fossil CO_2 includes emissions from coal, oil, gas, flaring, cement, steel, and other industrial processes. Fossil emissions do not include land use change, deforestation, soils, or vegetation.

Figure 7.1 Per capita CO_2 emissions, 2021
Source: Ritchie et al. (2020); OurWorldInData (2023). 'CO_2 and Greenhouse Gas Emissions'. Published online at OurWorldInData.org. Retrieved from: https://ourworldindata.org/co2-and-other-greenhouse-gas-emissions [Online Resource]

global south – a condition that Farhana Sultana (2022) describes as 'climate coloniality'. This condition, Sultana (2022) argues, arises through the interlinkages of global development, capitalism, colonialism, and geopolitics that reproduce 'global governance structures, discursive framings [and] imagined solutions' that perpetuate current practices of extractivism and dispossession.

Factor in the power and influence of key lobbyists from extractive and other industries, as well as the unremitting quest for economic growth as a sign of progress, and some of the barriers to tackling climate change and realising sustainable global development become quickly evident. Yet there is hope and – albeit very limited – time to make changes to reduce greenhouse gas emissions. Previous successes with tackling global environmental concerns with acid rain and the hole in the ozone layer suggest that international political consensus and action can be mobilised. However, such efforts – including to support transitions to low-carbon energy systems – must avoid being neo-colonialist and must incorporate the agency, knowledges, and values of local communities to realise socially and environmentally just solutions (Barragan-Contreras, 2023).

Previous efforts to reduce carbon emissions and increase carbon capture have had limited successes. The promotion of 'carbon offsetting' remains common but problematic. Typically involving the planting of trees to 'capture' the equivalent carbon emissions from a journey or production process (the 'net zero' approach to carbon), critics highlight how these projects are linked to land enclosures in equatorial regions (potentially displacing communities and undermining local livelihoods – all to allow the wealthy to continue to salve their conscience without changing their lifestyles). At a larger scale, the REDD+ policy from the 2007 Bali conference and then reaffirmed as part of the Paris Climate Agreement sought to Reduce Emissions from Deforestation and forest Degradation (REDD+). This policy envisioned forests as key to addressing climate change – both through reducing deforestation (and associated carbon emissions) and through supporting reforestation and managing existing forests. Initially linked to the carbon cap-and-trade market (carbon cap = limit on the amount of greenhouse gas emissions which was to be reduced over time; carbon trade = essentially a commodity exchange whereby companies/countries can buy and sell emissions 'credits'), this approach has been piecemeal and poorly funded. More broadly, REDD+ activities have included small-scale, community-level efforts to reduce deforestation (e.g. for charcoal burning) and promote reforestation, as well as efforts to reduce large-scale deforestation for logging, cattle ranching, and palm oil plantations.

The limited successes (and controversies surrounding) carbon credits and carbon capture (including through REDD+ schemes) indicate that much remains to be done in reducing carbon emissions, preventing the triggering of so-called 'carbon bombs' (major fossil fuel projects that would release vast quantities of carbon dioxide), and ensuring we don't pass certain 'tipping points' which would trigger knock-on or domino-like greenhouse gas emissions (such as the melting of the Arctic permafrost). Unless climate change is addressed urgently, these changes will have increasingly severe knock-on effects on other global development concerns including climate-related migration, the unequal burden of the effects and costs of climate change (which are forecast to disproportionately affect the global south), increasing inequalities, crop failures and food shortages, and so on.

THE GLOBAL COMMONS

As states seek to drive economic growth, increasing efforts are being made to exploit resources located in the deep ocean and polar regions. The potential for significant direct environmental damage from such resource exploitation activities is enormous – potentially disrupting or destroying fragile ecosystems and biodiversity. Beyond these direct impacts, key global development challenges are likely to grow in relation to air and water quality, pollution, and access. The negative health and social impacts of air pollution are already well documented, as are the impacts of water shortages on crop yields and subsistence livelihoods in many regions, while geopolitical and other tensions are growing in relation to access to and extraction from trans-national water sources.

In short, the global commons – atmosphere, water, biodiversity, biomes, polar regions, deep oceans – are vital for human survival, but they are facing mounting threats and undergoing rapid damage from human actions. As it stands, 'seventy-five percent of Earth's land surface has been significantly altered, 66 per cent of the ocean area is experiencing increasing cumulative impacts, and over 85 per cent of wetlands has been lost' (UN, 2019: xxix). There is mounting concern that if one system fails, we risk a chain-reaction that will tip other systems over the edge. Linked to this is a need to focus on preventing biomes and other systems reaching 'tipping points': the point at which irreversible changes occur in a part of the world's biosphere and which may then lead to cascading negative outcomes. For instance, there is mounting concern with global warming leading to a melting of the Arctic permafrost. This frozen ground holds massive stores of greenhouse gases which would be released if the ground thaws. In turn, this would lead to an acceleration of warming and further (and faster) melting – and so the vicious cycle would continue. Other tipping points are to do with sea temperatures and polar ice – if temperatures increase beyond a specific point, the melting of sea ice and the polar ice caps would irreversibly speed up, leading to biome changes and alterations to ocean circulations causing further disruptions to bio-diversity but also climate and natural hazards.

Moving forwards, sustainable global development will increasingly rely upon a strengthening of international governance structures and institutions to avoid inter-state resource-related conflicts. With the rise of nativist politics and resurgent nationalism in many states and increasing tensions between major world political and economic powers, the potential for increased global cooperation seems limited at present. Yet the need for effective institutions which can develop and – crucially, as this is largely missing at present – enforce legally binding treaties to realise sustainability in global development is clear.

GEOPOLITICAL CHANGES

Geopolitics, political power, and security interests remain at the heart of global development agendas and practice. The shifting geopolitical landscape resulting from China's increasing economic and political power is challenging the dominance of Western donors and the Bretton Woods Institutions. China's emergence as a major source of development funding, most ambitiously through the current Belt and Road Initiative, has resulted in various countries adopting a 'look East' strategy in seeking development funding. Lacking the baggage of colonialism and without the same conditionalities attached, China is becoming the funder of choice for many states, while building China's 'soft power' and strategic access to natural resources.

Growing concerns in the West regarding China's military posturing, Russia's invasion of Ukraine, and growing geopolitical tensions more widely linked to a potential shift to a new 'world order' all have implications for global development. On the one hand, these are evident in shifts to the global development funding landscape. On the other, it should be expected that as geopolitical tensions rise we will see a further intensification in the 'securitisation' of development aid while global development aid budgets come under pressure as (donor) states increase their levels of spending on defence budgets.

TECHNOLOGY AND CONSUMPTION

At the heart of many pronouncements on global development is a large degree of techno-optimism. From the Brundtland Commission to the present day, future technologies are held up as a magic bullet that will support continued economic growth while reducing environmental impacts. In other contexts, techno-optimists have argued that ICTs will support democratisation, expand access to education, support economic growth and employment, and deliver myriad other benefits.

Advances in technology have supported increases in life expectancy, delivered more efficient ways of capturing and storing 'green' energy, and supported spaces of political participation and social networking. However, this reliance on techno-optimism or technology as the solution to sustainable development is misguided. Online spaces can be beneficial for promoting democratic ideals, but can also be subject to intensive surveillance and be used as an oppressive space for regressive purposes. Smart phones, tablets, laptops, electric cars, and other devices can have all sorts of benefits for global development – but they also come at a cost: the environmental costs of mining for precious minerals and metals, the exploitation of workers and denial of basic rights within the production chain, the pollution from not only the production of these devices but also their disposal.

Then there are the environmental impacts of our use of technologies directly – from vehicular pollution to the energy consumption of air conditioning units. As demand for and access to technologies grow, so too will the environmental impacts of their use – often exacerbating the very issues they were designed to address (as in the case of air conditioning). While steps are slowly being taken to tackle some of these costs, including addressing the in-built obsolescence of some electronic devices, there is a long way to go not only in the introduction of more sustainability-orientated policies but also with regards to our own consumption behaviours.

What we each consume has a bearing on global development – whether the environmental and human costs of fast fashion, of upgrading to the latest mobile phone, or of our dietary choices. The obsession with economic growth means we are constantly asked to consume – and consume more. Globally, our level of consumption is already deeply unsustainable: we are using nature 1.8 times faster than it can regenerate (or, in other words, we need 1.8 planet Earths to meet current consumption levels). Unsurprisingly, there are huge variations in consumption levels between countries – from Qatar and Luxembourg (if everyone on Earth consumed at the levels of these countries we would need 9 and 8.2 Earths respectively) through Canada, the UAE, and USA (5.1 Earths) and Italy and Chile (2.7 Earths) to Benin, Jamaica, and Sri Lanka (1 Earth), Rwanda, Pakistan, and Mozambique (0.5 Earths), and finally Yemen (0.3 Earths) (Earthovershootday, 2022). One of the fundamental challenges to sustainable global development is how to achieve development while reducing the rate at which we consume nature – a particular conundrum given the emphasis on development as economic growth and that wealthier nations consume more. In response to this, we see the rise of campaigns to 'maintain and repair' and the introduction of legislation to prohibit in-built obsolescence of appliances and gadgets, from televisions to mobile phones.

DECOLONISING DEVELOPMENT

Integral to efforts to achieve sustainable and just outcomes for both people and the planet is the need to challenge the innate Eurocentrism of development studies and practice. Such efforts are vital not only to problematising how the world is viewed and known, but also in thinking about what development is and how it is defined and measured. As Barragan-Contreras (2023) argues, it is imperative that the sector productively engages with local and indigenous knowledges, cultures, and ways-of-being to realise a more 'just' form of development and to disrupt power dynamics in talking about and defining development and the global south (McEwan, 2009).

For those working within the global development sector, this also means a commitment to tackling racism and the prevalence of 'white saviourism' which remains entrenched (BOND 2021) and is entwined with recent abuse scandals. More widely, this requires scholars, policy makers, practitioners, donors/funders, politicians, and institutional officials to critically acknowledge not only the historical connections between colonialism and the creation of 'development', but how these histories continue to frame and permeate development agendas and practices today. From this starting point, concerted efforts are then needed to change ways of knowing about and doing global development in order to rebalance power relations and decentre Western-centric approaches to development.

(HOW) CAN WE ACHIEVE *SUSTAINABLE* GLOBAL DEVELOPMENT?

Underpinning many of the key concerns noted already, and perhaps crucial for thinking about what the post-2030 global development policy landscape may look like, is the question of how to achieve *sustainable development*. It seems clear that the techno-optimism of the Brundtland Commission Report is fundamentally flawed. It is also clear that the current normalised logic of capitalist accumulation is inherently destructive, and – for all efforts and claims to the contrary – the continued reliance upon economic growth as the means, ends, and measurement of development is unsustainable. What then might the radical (if longstanding) alternative be?

SUSTAINABILITY WITHOUT ECONOMIC GROWTH

A key premise of global development agendas has continually been the emphasis on economic growth as the driver for development. This stance was, as mentioned earlier, core to the Brundtland

Commission Report in 1987 and remains central to the SDGs. Has the time now come, as 'degrowth' advocates have long argued, for us to drop the obsession with economic growth as *the* development solution?

The world economy has – and continues – to grow. But development challenges remain – and, in many cases, are getting worse. In short, the current economic growth model has continually benefited the few, at the expense of the majority: the promise of wealth and riches for all is essentially a chimera within the current dominant economic model. The primary focus upon GDP as a measure of growth and development however means that economic growth becomes not the means to an end, but an end in and of itself.

As a result, concerns over inequalities, human rights, social justice, environmental protection, gender, delivery of quality social services, and so on are all overtaken by the focus on economic growth. As outlined earlier, a degrowth approach would use social and environmental well-being (using indicators such as happiness) as measures of prosperity and development. Whether or not such an approach will be politically acceptable to governments within our lifetimes is doubtful. However, it does help us to think about more specific policies and approaches that may be stepping-stones on a journey towards genuinely sustainable global development.

The first is to acknowledge that both global and national economic inequalities are key barriers to development. There is, in short, more than enough wealth to ensure everyone can have a reasonable standard of living. The problem is that both wealth and income are distributed in a vastly skewed and distorted manner, and these discrepancies are widening. There is a clear and compelling need for a progressive approach to wealth redistribution and income taxation at both national and international levels (Chancel et al., 2022). This argument is not one confined to left-leaning politicians – we have seen growing numbers of the ultra-wealthy openly calling upon governments to increase the taxes they pay to support development agendas.

Various arguments and suggestions have been made as to specific ways to begin to move towards a more progressive taxation approach, including increasing tax rates on higher levels of personal income and/or wealth, increasing taxes on corporations, introducing taxes on currency and other financial transactions (often called 'Tobin' or 'Robin Hood' taxes), and on the digital sector. Without international agreements, however, key challenges remain as wealthy individuals and corporations utilise offshore accounts and other mechanisms to realise 'tax efficiencies'. In short, realising a fairer and more progressive international economic system – not only in relation to taxation but also ensuring global trading systems are fair and that global development spending is used to create enabling environments for development – is vital to support sustainable global development (Glennie, 2021). Despite this, the chances of such international cooperation and agreement being reached are negligible.

Compounding this situation is the issue of temporality. While political leaders are increasingly talking about pressing needs for sustainability, the reality is that their own (political) sustainability remains primarily determined by much shorter election cycles. This means (political) self-interest limits the willingness of elected leaders to make the radical changes needed to realise the urgent and fundamental shifts required to realise environmental sustainability.

INTERNATIONAL COOPERATION FOR SUSTAINABILITY

Sustainable global development cannot be realised at a national level alone. It requires international cooperation and solidarity. Unfortunately, it feels as if both are in increasingly short supply. Governments seem to be withdrawing from or reneging on international agreements relating to human rights or climate change. In other situations, we have seen how nationalist self-interest led to 'vaccine nationalism' and the hoarding of Covid-19 vaccine doses by wealthy countries. By early October 2021, more than 70% of residents in Malta, Spain, Denmark, Qatar, the UAE, Canada, and various other countries were fully vaccinated against Covid-19, while less than 1% of the population were fully vaccinated in many African states including Chad, Niger, Uganda, Nigeria, and Tanzania (see Table 7.1).

The legacies of the Covid-19 pandemic for global development are profound – not only in casting a harsh light on national self-interest and vaccine nationalism, but in pushing between 88 and 115 million people into severe poverty (Ratha et al., 2020), curtailing remittance flows, and severely stretching national budgets. The effects and

Table 7.1 Percentage of population vaccinated against Covid-19, 2021

	Fully	*Partially*	*Not*
South America	42	20	38
North America	48	10	42
Europe	52	4.4	43
Asia	37	15	48
Oceania	34	16	50
Africa	4.5	2.4	97.1

Source: Data from https://ourworldindata.org/covid-vaccinations (retrieved 04/10/2021) – Coronavirus (COVID-19) Vaccinations

outcomes of knock-on effects in relation to increased health-care costs, disruption to education, migrant working patterns, and myriad other aspects of everyday life are only now beginning to be understood – but will be integral to global development agendas in the coming years.

Ultimately, to realise genuinely sustainable global development not only do we need to rethink how we measure 'development' and 'progress', we also need to overcome nationalist imperatives. International cooperation and collaboration are needed not only to recognise and acknowledge both historical and contemporary causes and outcomes of inequalities, but also to collectively agree and commit to legally binding commitments to protect the global commons, tackle the causes and outcomes of climate change, pursue progressive strategies to reduce inequalities at national and international levels, and more.

Without this international commitment and solidarity, we are doomed to repeat the mistakes of the past. In short, global challenges require global solutions – and the only way to realise this is through global cooperation and partnerships.

REFERENCES

Barragan-Contreras, S. (2023). Towards more pluralistic energy justice frameworks. In Bouzarovski, S., Fuller, S., Reames, T. (eds) *Handbook on Energy Justice.* Cheltenham: Edward Elgar.

Bierbaum, R.M., Fay, M., Ross-Larson, B. (2010). *World Development Report 2010: Development and Climate Change.* Washington, DC: World Bank Group.

BOND (2021). *Racism, Power and Truth: Experiences of People of Colour in Development*. London: BOND.

Chancel, L., Piketty, T., Saez, E., Zucman, G. (2022). *World Inequality Report 2022*. Paris: World Inequality Lab, UNDP.

Earthovershootday (2022). How many earths or countries do we need? https://www.overshootday.org/how-many-earths-or-countries-do-we-need/ (retrieved 01/08/2022).

Glennie, J. (2021). *The Future of Aid: Global Public Investment*. Abingdon: Routledge.

Hammett, D., Jackson, L. (2021). The new age of the nation state? *Geography*, 106 (2): 76–84.

Intergovernmental Panel on Climate Change (IPCC) (2022). *Climate Change 2022: Impacts, Adaptation and Vulnerability*. Geneva: IPCC. https://www.ipcc.ch/report/ar6/wg2/ (retrieved 20/03/2023).

McEwan, C. (2009). *Postcolonialism and Development*. Abingdon: Routledge.

Moyo, D. (2009). *Dead Aid: Why Aid is Not Working and How There is Another Way for Africa*. London: Penguin.

OurWorldInData (2023). CO2 emissions per capita. Oxford: Global Change Data Lab. https://ourworldindata.org/grapher/co-emissions-per-capita (retrieved 04/01/2023).

Ratha, D., De, S., Kim, E.J., Plaza, S., Seshan, G., Yameogo, N.D. (2020). *Migration and Development Brief 33: Phase II: COVID-19 Crisis through a Migration Lens*. Washington, DC: KNOMAD-World Bank.

Ritchie, H., Roser, M., Rosado, P. (2020). CO2 and greenhouse gas emissions. Oxford: Global Change Data Lab. https://ourworldindata.org/co2-and-other-greenhouse-gas-emissions (retrieved 04/01/2023).

Sultana, F. (2022). The unbearable heaviness of climate coloniality. *Political Geography*, 99, 102638.

UN (2019). *The Future is Now: Science for Achieving Sustainable Development – Global Sustainable Development Report 2019*. New York: United Nations.

INDEX

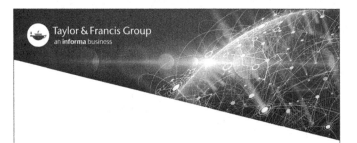

Printed in the United States
by Baker & Taylor Publisher Services